Payard
Cookies

Payard
Cookies

FRANÇOIS PAYARD *with* ANNE E. MCBRIDE

PHOTOGRAPHY BY ROGÉRIO VOLTAN

HOUGHTON MIFFLIN HARCOURT
BOSTON / NEW YORK / 2015

For my father, who gave me my love of cookies, and so much more

For information about permission to reproduce selections from this book, write to
Permissions, Houghton Mifflin Harcourt Publishing Company, 215 Park Avenue South,
New York, New York 10003.

www.hmhco.com

Library of Congress Cataloging-in-Publication Data
Payard, François.
    Payard cookies / François Payard with Anne E. McBride ; photography by
Rogério Voltan.
        pages cm
    Includes index.
    ISBN 978-0-544-51298-6 (hardcover); 978-0-544-51386-0 (ebook)
1.   Cookies. 2. Cooking, French. I. McBride, Anne E. II. Title.
TX772.P339 2015
641.86'54—dc23
2014044010

Jacket & book design by Rita Sowins / Sowins Design

Printed in China
C&C 10 9 8 7 6 5 4 3 2 1

Introduction

Cookies are what my family loves the most. That's really saying something, considering that we are a multi-generational family of pastry chefs. I grew up in the south of France, where we eat a lot of ice cream rather than elaborate desserts, since it's so hot. And what better to dip into your ice cream than a cookie? My dad, who was a pastry chef, always skipped dessert but would never skip eating a cookie. His favorite ones were sablés and similar "dry" cookies that can be used to scoop up ice cream and as a result soften ever so slightly. He rotated a selection of fifteen to twenty cookies in his pastry shop, making a huge batch of a different variety every day, since most cookies keep well for several days. This was a great way to increase sales since he also sold frozen cakes that were nicely complemented by the cookies—something he always pointed out to his customers. What is available every day also becomes less tempting or even enjoyable, so the ever-rotating selection of cookies made for treats he enjoyed greatly, as did the regulars of his pastry shop, who never knew what might await them when they stepped inside.

The rich and buttery financiers my father made in a large barquette size were his best-sellers. After he retired, he still made them at home for my sister, since they were her favorite, and would often have some in the freezer, ready for one of us to visit. He passed away in spring 2014, and it was a bittersweet moment when my family was all together again a few months later and we ate the very last batch of financiers he ever made. Being able to share his recipe here means that others will make this their special cookie—the best possible way to honor my father's memory.

I am proud and happy to share many of his recipes in this book, since I grew up with them and they have meant so much to me for so long, bringing back childhood memories with just one bite. Alongside these family favorites you will find dozens of cookie recipes that I developed over the years for my retail and wholesale businesses, and just for pleasure too. While mostly French and classic, they reflect my life in America and my deep appreciation of other European cookie traditions, like German and Swiss—I think that those, alongside the French, are the best cookies in the world. I've also spent two decades in New York, so Italian-American cookies are part of my repertoire too now.

In France, we very often buy cookies at pastry shops, knowing exactly which one does financiers or petits fours best and who has great specialties. A platter of cookies adds a nice touch, a little something extra, at the end of the meal and invites lingering around the table with a cup of coffee or a glass of grappa. In the United States, most cookie baking or purchasing seems to take place around the holidays, as part of special occasion celebrations. What I want to do with this book is give you a reason and an opportunity to make every day just a little more special. You can serve cookies on tiered platters (look for beautiful vintage ones at flea markets and in vintage shops, for example), on ceramic plates that have a more rustic appearance, on long rectangular or oblong serving plates, or really on anything that you'd like. One of the things I love most about cookies is that they allow a lot of self-expression, from flavor design to eating selection. So follow baking rules to ensure the recipes succeed, but other than that feel free to break any rules when it comes to serving.

The French way of making cookies consists of building layer after layer, starting by creaming butter and flour to create a sandier texture that is very enjoyable in the mouth. We typically break cookies into three categories in France: the "soft," or *moelleux*, ones, like financiers; the "dry," or *sec* ones, like sablés; and the "fresh" petits fours, which are akin to mini pastries. Here I focus on the first two kinds. When serving a cookie platter, you want to offer a range of textures, flavors, and shapes to keep it as interesting as possible. This book is organized in a way that lets you pick from the different categories easily.

We sell a lot of cookies at Payard, focusing mostly on classic varieties. We used to bake 500 pounds a day for our wholesale business, and also sold some in bulk in the stores so that customers could come in and, as they might have in my dad's shop, pick from a rotating assortment. While we no longer sell cookies in bulk, we nonetheless always have available bags of certain types of cookies, not to mention a wide selection of macarons. Our best-sellers are always financiers (pistachio, apricot, chocolate, and vanilla), followed by sablés and other dry and nutty cookies. We also always carry special cookies for Passover, which have the advantage of being gluten-free and are great to eat year-round.

My own favorites are sablés and every sort of crumbly cookie, along with my own style of biscotti, which I slice very thinly. I like traditional and simple flavors for cookies— the types you love and always go back to. Before bed you don't crave a curry-flavored chocolate, for example, but something simpler; it's the same with cookies. A few recipes in this book depart from this perspective, but it's generally my approach and preference when deciding what cookies to offer at the store or to bake for family and friends. Classic cookies also are not seasonal—even if some are more typically found around the holidays, and spiced cookies might be better matched to colder weather while light and jammy ones are perfect in summer breezes—which works well with my philosophy of eating cookies year-round. Cookies are the perfect one- or two-bite treats; they don't require a huge gastronomic commitment the way a slice of cake or pie might. When hosting a dinner party, I like to present a variety of cookies on a platter for that reason. Even someone who is not hungry for a full dessert will be happy to be able to enjoy one small sweet taste.

Create your own family traditions around cookies, going beyond the holidays and inviting your kids, partners, or friends to join you in the kitchen to bake together, or simply by sharing with them what you've baked. Bring cookie platters to work or give a friend an elegant bag or box filled with cookies. Learn to decorate beautiful cookies. Find your own specialty that will always be in your freezer. And join me in making every day just a little sweeter by baking more cookies.

Notes on Baking

❖ Ovens vary widely, which is why baking times are indicated in ranges. Generally, because they are small, cookies bake quickly. Don't go too far after you put a batch in the oven, and keep a close eye on them to monitor changes in appearance that indicate they are done. The first time you make a recipe is particularly important. Make your own notes in the margins of the book if you realize that in your oven, a cookie takes 11 minutes consistently, rather than an indicated range of 12 to 14, for example. And if you change ovens, keep an eye out again and adjust the range to one that is best for you.

❖ The yield of the cookies indicated by each recipe might vary slightly when you make them. Piping takes a lot of practice, for example, and you might not pipe all of your cookies as evenly or regularly as I do. Or you might cut them slightly thicker or thinner than the thickness I specify. You can reroll your dough trimmings and make more cookies, where applicable. Since each recipe makes a large amount of cookies, you will have plenty even if it's not the exact amount I specify.

❖ Cool the cookies on a cooling rack so you can reuse the baking sheet for more batches. If not specified, it doesn't matter whether you let them cool on the baking sheet or on a rack.

❖ You can freeze the dough, well wrapped in plastic and stored in a reusable plastic container so that it doesn't take on any odors—that's important—for up to a month.

❖ Some filling recipes will make a little extra caramel, ganache, or buttercream. All those keep well in the fridge.

❖ You might notice slight variations in equivalents of ingredients between grams and cups, when a little more or less won't make a difference to the recipe. But to the extent possible, bake by measuring in grams: It's so much easier, and scales are inexpensive now.

❖ When making dipped or glazed cookies, the length of time it will take for them to dry will depend on the temperature and humidity level of the room, which will vary by season. Use the time indications I give you as an average, not an absolute.

Equipment

Cookies don't require too many specialty ingredients, but you'll need a few pieces, from cookie cutters to pastry tips, that you might not have on hand already. All of these items are available in kitchenware stores or online, as listed in Resources (page 266).

BAKING SHEETS

You should have at least two baking sheets, preferably four. If you have four, you don't need to wait until the first two have cooled to finish baking the next batch of cookies, for example. Most of the recipes here use standard 10½-by-15-inch rimmed baking sheets, but keep at least one larger, such as a 13-by-18-inch sheet, on hand too. Baking sheets are also very useful when organizing your work space and to transport filled molds, particularly silicone molds (such as those for financiers), which can be flimsy, in and out of the refrigerator or oven.

COOKIE CUTTERS

You should invest in a box of assorted sizes of round cookie cutters, either plain or scalloped, which can be the default shape of any cookies and are used frequently in this book. A star-shaped cutter is also great to have on hand. Then have fun with other shapes, looking for particularly distinctive ones when you travel, for example. If you want to immediately increase your collection, pick up some of the shapes used in the Calendar of Cookies (pages 240 to 263).

COOLING RACKS

Most cookies can be transferred from the baking sheet to a cooling rack to cool to room temperature. When they should cool on the baking sheet, the recipe specifies it. Transferring the cookies to a rack allows you to reuse the baking sheet to bake more from the same batch. Choose large rectangular cooling racks that can fit at least the same number of cookies as your baking sheet.

MEASURING CUP

A large glass liquid measuring cup, going up to 4 cups, is useful not only to measure larger amounts of liquids, but also to pour batters into molds, such as when making financiers or mini cakes.

MOLDS AND PANS

Some of the specialty molds used in this book include cannelé, financier, and madeleine molds, as well as mini muffin pans. Most of these are available in kitchenware stores or online. Some of these cannot be substituted with any other molds, but I've indicated possible substitutions in each recipe where appropriate. Many specialty molds are available in silicone; because those are flexible, it is best to place them on a baking sheet before they go into the oven.

OFFSET METAL SPATULAS

When making cookies, metal spatulas are useful to remove delicate ones from the baking sheet after they have cooled. You might already have a large one on hand if you make a lot of cakes, but I like a small one and a medium one for cookies.

PARCHMENT PAPER

Parchment paper is essential when baking; for cookies it is most often used to line baking sheets, making for an easier cleanup job. It also allows you to slide the cookies onto a cooling rack and reuse the baking sheet to bake the next batch. Buy the unbleached kind. When cookies or their components do need to rest on paper but are not going in the oven, use waxed paper instead, which is less expensive. Many cookies that are iced, dipped in chocolate, or sticky should be stored with parchment or waxed paper between layers to keep them from sticking.

PIPING COOKIE DOUGH AND ROYAL ICING DECORATIONS

You will use pastry bags and tips to pipe both cookie dough and royal icing decorations. When piping, hold the bag near its middle rather than its top, so that you will have control over the pressure you exert to pipe the dough or the icing. Don't overfill the bag. Never refrigerate dough before piping it, or it will become too firm to pipe. When piping *gommés* (pages 119 to 122), the dough should be warm, or you'll break the bag when pressing on it. You can always let piped cookies rest on the baking sheet before you bake them, but avoid letting a dough that needs to be piped rest for too long in the bowl (the length of time it takes for one batch to bake is fine, since it's usually quick). Use a star pastry tip to make star-, shell-, and flower-shaped cookies or to give some added elements to a cookie piped in a straight line. Round tips give you solid shapes or lines. For royal icing, use small, fine round tips.

PASTRY BAGS OR RESEALABLE PLASTIC BAGS

Pastry bags allow you to pipe batter cleanly into financier molds or mini muffin pans, for example, or, fitted with a pastry tip, to pipe dough into shapes or create royal icing decorations. If you are out of pastry bags, use a resealable plastic bag and snip off one of its corners. Some doughs in the book are too stiff for plastic pastry bags, so you should also invest in a thicker fabric one.

PASTRY TIPS

Pastry tips are used with pastry bags, or they can be fitted to resealable plastic bags as well. For many purposes, cutting off the tip or corner of the bag will suffice to pipe a dough, but certain cookies require specific tips, and so do precise applications like cookie decorating. A couple of different sizes of star and round tips will carry you a long way— have at least a ½-inch and 1-inch tip of each kind for piping batters and doughs, plus smaller ones for decorating.

SCALE

Do me a favor and please buy a kitchen scale for baking, so that you can weigh all your ingredients rather than use a measuring cup (although I do include cup measures in this book, so you can make the recipes either way). You can find inexpensive scales online and in any superstore.

SILICONE BAKING MATS

Silicone baking mats, preferably Silpat, which are the best nonstick mats on the market, can be used instead of parchment paper to keep cookies, for example, from sticking to a baking sheet. They are reusable and can go from freezer to oven and then to the dishwasher without being affected by cold or heat.

SILICONE OR RUBBER SPATULAS

Spatulas are essential in a pastry kitchen. You will use them to fold or stir ingredients and to transfer a dough into a pastry bag for piping, for example. Silicone spatulas are preferable because they can withstand very high temperatures.

THERMOMETERS

A couple of recipes in this book call for a candy thermometer, for applications with sugar that can't be eyeballed, such as caramel or syrup for meringue. A candy thermometer can clip to the side of a pan, which allows you to monitor the progress of the sugar as it cooks.

Ingredients

Most of the recipes in this book use straightforward, easily available ingredients. Here are a few specialty ingredients that deserve a little more explanation.

ALMOND FLOUR

Almond flour is a staple of the French pastry kitchen. I use it all the time for everything from cakes to cookies. It gives the dough a light texture and a great almond flavor. You can purchase it (see Resources, page 266) or make your own by grinding blanched almonds very finely in a food processor, being careful not to turn them into a paste. There'll be about a 20 percent loss when grinding whole almonds into flour, so if you need 100 grams of flour, for example, grind about 120 grams of whole almonds (1⅓ cups whole almonds will give you about 1 cup of almond flour). Some stores sell unblanched almond flour, which will work just as well but might give a more rustic, speckled appearance to your cookies.

BUTTER

Always use unsalted butter and add salt separately, for more control over the flavor of your product. To cream the butter well, cut it into small pieces before placing it in the bowl of the stand mixer. The butter should be at room temperature but not to the point of melting.

CANDIED CITRUS PEEL

Candied orange, lemon, or grapefruit peel can be added to a wide variety of cookies, as you'll discover throughout the book. You will find a recipe on page 120, but you can also purchase them ready-made if you prefer (see Resources, page 266). Look for high-quality, natural (that is, without artificial colorants) candied citrus peels.

CANDIED GINGER

Like citrus peels, ginger is candied by being boiled, and then cooled, in sugar syrup. It adds a little spiciness and zing to the cookies in which it is included—only a few here, but feel free to add it wherever you'd like. Look for it in the baking section of higher-end supermarkets or gourmet food shops. It is sometimes called crystallized ginger.

CHOCOLATE

When filling or dipping cookies, I like using a chocolate that contains between 60 and 66 percent cacao. Valrhona's Caraïbe 66 percent cacao has a complex fruity and roasted flavor that works particularly well with cookies, but you can use any brand you like. It is available in bars and pistoles (small pieces), which are great for melting since you don't need to chop the chocolate. When tempering chocolate (see page 18), it is essential to use couverture chocolate, available at specialty stores (see Resources, page 266, for other sources). Regular chocolate will have a good flavor but lack shine.

Melting Chocolate

You can melt chocolate in the microwave or on the stovetop over a double boiler. The key is to make sure that no water touches the chocolate at any time, or it will cause it to seize. In that regard, the microwave is a bit safer. When using the microwave, however, melt the chocolate in short increments, stirring in between each, to ensure that the chocolate melts evenly and does not burn.

To melt chocolate in the microwave, place the chopped chocolate in a microwave-safe bowl. Microwave it on high power for 30 seconds, then remove it and stir. Return it to the microwave for another 15 seconds, remove, and stir. Repeat until the chocolate is completely melted. Stirring the chocolate will help it all melt, so make sure to let the residual heat and the stirring do their jobs before deciding whether the chocolate needs more time in the microwave. Otherwise, the chocolate that has already melted might thicken too much. The total time will depend on the quantity of chocolate you are melting. If only a little bit of chocolate is still hard, reduce the time in the microwave to 10 seconds.

To melt chocolate over a double boiler, fill a medium pot one-third full with water and bring it to a gentle simmer over medium heat. Place the chopped chocolate in a bowl that will fit snugly on top of the pot but not touch the water. Reduce the heat to low and place the bowl over the pot. Stir occasionally until the chocolate is melted.

Note: You can also use the double-boiler method to reheat ganaches and glazes that have cooled and thickened, or to finish melting chocolate for a ganache if the hot cream or milk that was poured over it did not melt it completely.

Tempering Chocolate

Several recipes in this book call for dipping cookies in melted chocolate. Although it is not 100 percent essential, the finished chocolate will have a much shinier appearance and crisper texture if you temper it first. Tempering is what gives chocolate its snap when you bite into it, and what allows the chocolate to set properly. If you do want to temper chocolate, the process consists of nothing more than melting couverture chocolate until it reaches a certain temperature, cooling it to a second temperature, and finally bringing it back up to and maintaining a slightly higher temperature, at which point you can work with it. This process binds the chocolate's crystals, which otherwise are somewhat "floating." A chocolate or instant-read thermometer is all that is needed. The chart below specifies the correct temperature for each stage for different types of chocolates. If it gets too cold, you have lost nothing more than time, and you can restart the process from the beginning. If it gets too hot, however, the chocolate can burn, resulting in an acrid taste and chocolate that may never set properly. Also make sure that absolutely no water makes contact with the chocolate, as even the smallest amount of water can cause it not to set properly.

TYPE OF CHOCOLATE	MELTING TEMPERATURE	COOLING TEMPERATURE	WORKING TEMPERATURE
Dark	122–131°F (50–55°C)	82–84°F (27.8–28.9°C)	87°F (30.5°C)
Milk	113–118°F (45–47.8°C)	80–82°F (26.7–27.8°C)	86°F (30°C)
White	113–118°F (45–47.8°C)	78–80°F (25.5–26.7°C)	84°F (28.9°C)

Only chocolate labeled as couverture can be tempered. It is not the type sold in most supermarkets, but you can find in high-end markets (such as Whole Foods), in baking supply stores, or online (see Resources, page 266). Couverture chocolate is of very high quality and contains more cocoa butter than what you see labeled as regular baking chocolate. It is already tempered, so melting it and tempering it is much easier. I normally use couverture chocolate pistoles, which do not need to be chopped to be melted.

Chocolate can be tempered multiple times without problems, so, since it is hard to temper small quantities of chocolate, it is best to work with a minimum of 1 pound; excess tempered chocolate can simply be allowed to set completely and retempered at a later time. The room in which you temper chocolate should be neither too warm nor too cold. Both extremes will make it hard for you to bring your chocolate into temper, or, if you manage, to keep it at the proper temperature for the time you'll need it to complete your recipe.

Although three methods exist to temper chocolate, this is the one I prefer. I chop the desired amount of chocolate and set one-third of it aside. I melt the bulk of the chocolate until it reaches the right melting temperature. I then stir in the reserved chocolate to bring it to its cooling temperature, and reheat the full amount of chocolate slightly until it reaches its working temperature. Here is the method in more detail:

PROCEDURES:

Start with 1 pound couverture chocolate of any type, finely chopped. Put one-third of the chocolate in a bowl, and set aside.

With a chocolate or instant-read thermometer handy, fill a medium pot one-third full with water and bring it to a gentle simmer over medium heat. Place the remaining two-thirds of the chocolate in a bowl that will fit snugly on top of the pot but not touch the water. Reduce the heat to low and place the bowl over the pot. Occasionally stir the chocolate gently with a silicone spatula until it is completely melted. Check its temperature regularly to make sure that you do not go above the desired temperature.

Alternatively, place the chopped chocolate in a microwave-safe bowl. Microwave it on high power for 15 seconds, then remove it and stir it with a silicone spatula. Return it to the microwave for another 15 seconds, remove, and stir. Repeat until the chocolate is completely melted.

Once the chocolate reaches the desired melting temperature, stir in the reserved chocolate to lower the chocolate to the cooling temperature. Once that temperature is reached, return the chocolate to the double boiler or to the microwave and briefly heat it until it reaches its working temperature.

Use the chocolate as indicated in the recipe. You can use the chocolate for about 5 to 10 minutes, then you will need to reheat it very briefly to bring it back to the right temperature, and stir it quickly as soon as it is off the heat to even out the temperature in the whole bowl. Reheat it over a pan of simmering water for 15 to 20 seconds or in the microwave for 10 seconds at a time (transferring the chocolate to a microwave-safe bowl if needed). Feel the temperature of the chocolate when you first temper it so that you can gauge the correct temperature when you reheat it.

Once you are finished, pour any leftover tempered chocolate into an airtight container, and let it solidify into a block. Temper it again as needed until you run out of it.

FLOUR

Cookies don't require a lot of gluten development. There is no need for elasticity in the dough; mixing it is just a matter of binding the ingredients. All-purpose flour thus works best for all the recipes in this book.

HONEY

I use clover honey in most recipes, but you should feel free to substitute your favorite kind where appropriate to give your cookies specific honey flavors.

NUTS

Whether you are using pecans, walnuts, or almonds, it's important in most recipes to toast nuts in order to fully develop their flavor and intensify the taste they bring to cookies like Pecan Squares (page 103), Pain Turc (page 111), and Spiced Nut Biscotti (page 213).

PROCEDURES:
Preheat the oven to 350°F (180°C).

Spread the nuts in a single layer on a baking sheet and place them in the oven for 10 to 12 minutes. Shake the pan a couple of times during the process, and watch the nuts carefully so they don't burn. Remove the nuts from the oven as soon as you start to smell them and they start to turn light brown. Transfer to a plate to cool. The nuts can be kept in an airtight container for up to 1 day.

PRALINE AND PISTACHIO PASTES

Praline paste is a puree of hazelnuts and sugar; pistachio paste, as its name indicates, uses ground pistachios. You can buy them both at gourmet grocery stores, specialty pastry retailers, or online (see Resources, page 266). You can also make them yourself using the recipes on pages 22 and 23.

Praline Paste

MAKES ABOUT 1 CUP (240 GRAMS)

Praline paste is typically made of an equal amount of almonds and hazelnuts, or with only almonds or only hazelnuts, that are cooked together in caramel and cooled on a large sheet, which is then processed into a paste. I also add hazelnut oil to intensify its flavor. You can make praline paste with any type of nuts, such as walnuts and peanuts, and even with sesame seeds; you can keep the ratio at equal amounts of almonds and other nuts or make it with only one type of nut.

---

1 tablespoon (13 grams) hazelnut or vegetable oil, plus extra for the pan

¾ cup (150 grams) granulated sugar

2 tablespoons (30 grams) water

½ cup (70 grams) blanched almonds, toasted (see page 21)

½ cup (70 grams) blanched hazelnuts, toasted (see page 21)

2 teaspoons (10 grams) pure vanilla extract (optional)

Brush a rimmed baking sheet with oil.

Place the sugar and water in a medium saucepan over medium-high heat, and bring to a boil. Stir to dissolve the sugar. If sugar sticks to the sides of the pot, dip a pastry brush in water and brush the sides. Cook until the sugar turns a light caramel color, 3 to 5 minutes.

Remove the pot from the heat (without turning it off) and stir in the almonds, hazelnuts, and vanilla, if using. Return the pot to the heat and cook, stirring, until the nuts are completely coated with caramel and the mixture turns a dark amber color.

Immediately pour the nut mixture onto the prepared baking sheet. Be careful not to let the caramel splatter, so that you don't get burnt. Let cool for 30 minutes, or until hard.

With a large chef's knife, coarsely chop the praline. Place the pieces in the bowl of a food processor and process for about a minute, until it reaches the consistency of sand. Add the oil and process for another 30 seconds, until the mixture turns into a paste. Transfer to an airtight container and refrigerate for up to 1 week.

Pistachio Paste

MAKES ABOUT 1²/₃ CUPS (390 GRAMS)

I add mint leaves to my pistachio paste to intensify the green color of the paste and enhance its flavor.

---

2 tablespoons (27 grams) vegetable oil, plus extra for the pan

¾ cup (150 grams) granulated sugar

2 tablespoons (30 grams) water

1²/₃ cups (190) grams shelled pistachios, toasted (see page 21)

2 teaspoons (10 grams) pure vanilla extract (optional)

8 fresh mint leaves

Follow the directions for Praline Paste (opposite), substituting the pistachios for the almonds and hazelnuts and adding the mint to the food processor right before the oil.

Buttery Cookies

Considering France's love story with butter in general, it's no surprise that my country has a rich tradition of buttery cookies, loved for their flaky and tender texture just as much as for their flavor. The cookies in this chapter are generally perfect accompaniments to a cup of tea or coffee and are easy to package as gifts. Some, like the Langues de Chat or Palets aux Raisins, are delicate small cookies, while the Sablés Bretons bake in a mini muffin pan and are sturdier as a result. Checkerboards are beautiful cookies that highlight the flavors of both orange and chocolate, for one of the most assertive cookies presented here. Coconut Stars allow you to be creative: You can make small stars indeed, or large ones, or just go wild with your favorite cookie cutter. Most of the doughs can be frozen, well wrapped in plastic and stored in a plastic container (to prevent other odors from permeating them), for up to a month, allowing you to bake just a few cookies at a time if you so wish. They bake quickly, so it'll be easy to make a few for an unexpected visit or craving.

Langues de Chat

Langues de chat *means "cat's tongues" in French; I like to think that it's because these cookies have a slightly rough texture but are soft and sweet. Flaky and buttery, this is a very classic French cookie that is great to serve with tea or coffee. It is a perfect platform for the flavor of vanilla since it contains few ingredients, but you can add the grated peel of one lemon to the dough if you'd like, for a citrusy variation.*

4 tablespoons (50 grams) unsalted butter, at room temperature

½ cup (65 grams) confectioners' sugar

1 large egg white

½ cup (65 grams) all-purpose flour

Pinch of salt

1 teaspoon (5 grams) pure vanilla extract

Preheat the oven to 350°F (180°C) and line a baking sheet with parchment paper.

In the bowl of a stand mixer fitted with the paddle attachment, beat the butter and confectioners' sugar together on low speed until the mixture becomes pale and fluffy. Add the egg white and mix until smooth. Add the flour and salt and continue mixing until the mixture is again smooth, then beat in the vanilla until it is fully incorporated.

With a spatula, transfer the dough to a pastry bag fitted with a ¼-inch round pastry tip. You can also just cut a ¼-inch opening into the tip of the pastry bag.

Pipe the dough onto the lined baking sheet in 2½-inch-long strips. Leave at least 1 inch between each cookie. Bake for 8 to 10 minutes, or until the edges of the cookies turn light brown but their centers remain a paler brown color.

Remove the cookies from the oven and let them cool completely on the baking sheet or a cooling rack, then store in an airtight container in a cool, dry place for up to 1 week.

> LANGUES DE CHAT, THIS PAGE, AND PALETS AUX RAISINS, PAGE 28

Palets aux Raisins

Palets aux Raisins (palet refers to their round shape) are close relatives of Langues de Chat (page 26). They share a crumbly texture and buttery taste, with the additional texture provided by plumped-up raisins. These cookies are meant to be tiny and delicate. The kick of their rum flavor makes them ideal to serve at the end of dinner. You can replace the rum with water if you prefer a nonalcoholic cookie.

⅓ cup (50 grams) raisins

3 tablespoons (40 grams) dark rum, such as Myers's

4 tablespoons (50 grams) unsalted butter, at room temperature

½ cup (50 grams) confectioners' sugar

1 large egg

½ cup (60 grams) all-purpose flour

Place the raisins and the rum in a microwave-safe container, cover with plastic wrap, and microwave for 1 minute. Carefully remove from the microwave and allow the raisins to steep in the covered bowl for at least 1 hour, or until they are plumped up. Drain the raisins before using and discard the liquid.

Preheat the oven to 350°F (180°C) and line a baking sheet with parchment paper.

In the bowl of a stand mixer fitted with the paddle attachment, beat the butter and confectioners' sugar together on low speed until the mixture becomes pale and fluffy. Add the egg and mix until smooth. Add the flour and mix until the dough is just combined.

With a spatula, transfer the dough to a pastry bag fitted with a ¼-inch round pastry tip. You can also just cut a ¼-inch opening into the tip of the pastry bag.

Pipe the dough onto the lined baking sheet in quarter-size rounds. Leave at least 1 inch between each cookie. Place a few raisins on top of each cookie. Bake for 8 to 10 minutes, or until the edges of the cookies turn light brown but their centers remain a paler brown color.

Remove the cookies from the oven and let them cool completely on the baking sheet or a cooling rack, then store in an airtight container in a cool, dry place for up to 1 week.

Galettes aux Noisettes

Hazelnut (noisette) flour is much more frequently used in France, and throughout western Europe, than in the United States, for all sorts of cakes and cookies, like these little rounds. It is simply ground blanched hazelnuts. If you grind them at home, it's fine if a bit of skin remains on the hazelnuts; it'll just give your cookies a more rustic look. Start with about 20 percent more whole hazelnuts than the amount of flour you need; here, about 1⅓ cups whole hazelnuts will yield the correct amount ground. Make sure that your hazelnut flour is fresh; if it is rancid or even just old, it will be greasier and the cookies will spread too much.

8 ounces plus 1 tablespoon (240 grams) unsalted butter, at room temperature

1 cup plus 2 tablespoons (100 grams) hazelnut flour

¾ cup (97 grams) all-purpose flour

½ cup (100 grams) granulated sugar

Pinch of salt

1 large egg yolk

In the bowl of a stand mixer fitted with the paddle attachment, beat the butter, hazelnut flour, all-purpose flour, sugar, and salt on low speed until combined. Add the egg yolk and mix on medium speed until combined. Shape the dough into a disk and wrap it well in plastic wrap. Refrigerate for at least 2 hours.

Preheat the oven to 325°F (160°C). Line a baking sheet with parchment paper.

Divide the dough in half, rewrap one half, and reserve it in the refrigerator. On a lightly floured work surface, roll out half the dough to a thickness of ¼ inch. Using a 2-inch round cookie cutter, cut out cookies and place them 1 inch apart on the prepared baking sheet. Reroll the scraps and cut out more cookies.

Bake the cookies for 12 to 15 minutes, or until golden brown. Remove the cookies from the oven, let them cool slightly on the baking sheet, then transfer them to a cooling rack. Repeat with the remaining dough. Store in an airtight container in a cool, dry place for up to 2 weeks.

Diamants

MAKES ABOUT 60 COOKIES

The name of this cookie comes from the sparkling appearance it gains by being rolled in granulated sugar—like a diamond. The sugar also adds a lovely crunch. If you prefer to use vanilla extract (only the pure kind!) instead of a bean, stir in 2 tablespoons (30 grams) when you add the egg yolks into the mixture. To collect the seeds of the vanilla bean, cut it in half and scrape each half with the back of a knife.

14 ounces (400 grams) unsalted butter, at room temperature

1⅓ cups (160 grams) confectioners' sugar

1 vanilla bean, seeds only

3 large egg yolks

3½ cups (450 grams) all-purpose flour

1 teaspoon (4 grams) salt

1 cup (200 grams) granulated sugar

In the bowl of a stand mixer fitted with the paddle attachment, beat the butter, confectioners' sugar, and vanilla seeds until fully combined. Add 2 of the egg yolks and mix until combined, then add the flour and salt and mix only until the dough just comes together. Be careful not to overmix.

Place the dough on a piece of plastic wrap and roll it into a log 2 inches in diameter. Multiple smaller logs are easier to work with than one long one. Twist the ends of each piece of plastic wrap as you would to wrap a candy to help you achieve an evenly round log. Freeze the dough for about 2 hours, or until the logs are chilled all the way through. You can freeze the logs, well wrapped in plastic and stored in an airtight container, for up to 1 month.

Preheat the oven to 350°F (180°C) and line a baking sheet with parchment paper.

Pour the remaining egg yolk into a bowl and break it up with a fork. Pour the granulated sugar into a dish that can accommodate the size of your logs. A small casserole dish or plastic container is ideal, or even a baking sheet lined with waxed paper.

With a pastry brush, brush a log with the egg yolk, then roll it in the granulated sugar until it is completely coated. Return it to the freezer for about 5 minutes, then slice the hardened log into ⅓-inch-thick slices, and place the slices on the lined baking sheet. Bake for 10 to 12 minutes, or until the cookies just begin to turn a light golden brown color.

Remove the cookies from the oven and transfer them to a cooling rack. Let them cool completely, then store them in an airtight container in a cool, dry place for up to 1 week.

Raspberry Diamants

MAKES ABOUT 40 COOKIES

I like to play with Diamants (page 30), which is such a traditional cookie, and invent my own variations, like this raspberry version. You can sandwich two of them with a little bit of peanut butter for a grown up PB&J, or with a little bit of jam. The pink color comes from food coloring. If you don't use it, your cookie will be paler than the photo depicts. At Payard, we use a special raspberry compound, but since it is not readily available to home cooks, I've adapted the recipe to work with raspberry jam (use the variety with seeds, since they contribute to the texture of the cookie). The cookie is slightly softer, since the jam contains sugar, but it's just as tasty. You can flavor it with any jam you'd like, but the seeds in the raspberry variety add crunch, and its acidity also remains after the cookies are baked.

14 tablespoons (200 grams) unsalted butter, at room temperature

⅔ cup (80 grams) confectioners' sugar

2 large egg yolks

¼ cup (60 grams) raspberry jam with seeds

3 drops liquid red food coloring

1¾ cups (225 grams) all-purpose flour

Pinch of salt

1 cup (200 grams) granulated sugar

In the bowl of a stand mixer fitted with the paddle attachment, beat the butter and confectioners' sugar until fully combined. Add 1 of the egg yolks, the raspberry jam, and the food coloring and mix until combined, then add the flour and salt and mix only until the dough just comes together. Be careful not to overmix.

Place the dough on a piece of plastic wrap and roll it into a log 1½ inches in diameter. Twist the ends of the plastic wrap as you would to wrap a candy to help you achieve an evenly round log. Freeze the dough for about 2 hours, or until the log is chilled all the way through. You can freeze the log, well wrapped in plastic and stored in an airtight container, for up to 1 month.

Preheat the oven to 350°F (180°C) and line a baking sheet with parchment paper.

Pour the remaining egg yolk into a bowl and break it up with a fork. Pour the granulated sugar into a dish that can accommodate the size of your log. A small casserole dish or plastic container is ideal, or even a baking sheet lined with waxed paper.

With a pastry brush, brush the log with the egg yolk, then roll it in the granulated sugar until it is completely coated. Return it to the freezer for about 5 minutes, then slice the hardened log into ¼-inch-thick slices, and place the slices on the lined baking sheet. Bake for 8 to 10 minutes, or until the cookies just begin to darken in color.

Remove the cookies from the oven and transfer them to a cooling rack. Let them cool completely, then store them in an airtight container in a cool, dry place for up to 1 week.

Cornmeal Cookies

MAKES ABOUT 50 COOKIES

These cookies contain cornmeal in addition to flour, which gives them a different flavor and texture than regular sablés—a bit of an American twist. For extra crunch, I like adding freeze-dried corn to the dough, which is simply corn kernels that have been frozen very rapidly at extremely cold temperatures to preserve their flavor and texture. You will find it at stores such as Whole Foods or Trader Joe's, but you can also omit it from the recipe.

8 ounces (225 grams) unsalted butter, at room temperature

1 cup plus 2 tablespoons (225 grams) granulated sugar

¾ cup (120 grams) cornmeal

5 large egg yolks

2½ cups (325 grams) all-purpose flour

½ teaspoon (2 grams) salt

¾ cup (23 grams) freeze-dried corn (optional)

Fleur de sel (optional)

In the bowl of a stand mixer fitted with the paddle attachment, beat the butter, sugar, and cornmeal together on low speed until well combined. Add 4 of the egg yolks, one at a time, waiting until each is well incorporated before adding the next. Add the flour, salt, and freeze-dried corn, if using, and mix only until the dough just comes together. Be careful not to overmix.

Divide the dough into thirds and place each piece on a piece of plastic wrap. Roll each piece of dough into a log 2 to 3 inches in diameter. Twist the ends of each piece of plastic wrap as you would to wrap a candy to help you achieve an evenly round log. Freeze for about 2 hours, or until the logs are chilled all the way through. You can freeze the logs for up to 1 month.

Preheat the oven to 350°F (180°C) and line a baking sheet with parchment paper.

With a sharp knife, cut the dough into ¼-inch-thick slices. Pour the remaining egg yolk into a bowl and break it up with a fork.

With a pastry brush, brush each cookie with a bit of egg yolk and top with a tiny pinch of fleur de sel, if using. Bake for 8 to 12 minutes, or until the cookies just begin to turn a light golden brown color.

Remove the cookies from the oven and transfer them to a cooling rack. Let them cool completely, then store them in an airtight container in a cool, dry place for up to 1 week.

Coconut Stars

This recipe makes a lot of little stars, but you can freeze both the dough and the finished cookies if you don't feel like making or eating them all at once. You can also cut the dough into your favorite shape and into larger sizes if you'd like—they might bake faster or slower depending on those factors, so just keep a close eye on them if you do that. They look like simple butter cookies, but biting into them reveals a delicate coconut flavor, further accentuated by the use of almond flour. It is bound to become one of the classic cookies you turn to any time you entertain or bring a treat, since they look so elegant presented on a tray or in a box or bag.

1 pound (487 grams) unsalted butter, at room temperature

2 cups (230 grams) confectioners' sugar

1 cup plus 2 tablespoons (112 grams) almond flour

1½ cups (112 grams) unsweetened desiccated coconut

1 teaspoon (5 grams) salt

2 large eggs

4½ cups plus ⅓ cup (487 grams) all-purpose flour

In the bowl of a stand mixer fitted with the paddle attachment, beat the butter and confectioners' sugar together on low speed until combined. Add the almond flour, coconut, and salt and mix until combined. Gradually add the eggs and mix until combined, then add the flour and mix only until the dough just comes together. Be careful not to overmix.

Remove the dough from the bowl, wrap it in plastic wrap, and refrigerate for about 2 hours, or until it is chilled all the way through. You can also freeze the dough, well wrapped in plastic and stored in an airtight container, for up to 1 month.

Preheat the oven to 350°F (180°C) and line two baking sheets with parchment paper.

On a floured surface, roll out the dough until it is slightly thinner than ¼ inch. Use a 1-inch star-shaped cookie cutter (or any shape you'd like) to cut the cookies, then transfer them to the lined baking sheets. Bake for about 8 minutes, or until the bottom edges of the cookies turn a very light golden brown. Repeat with the remaining dough until finished. You can reroll the scraps of cookie dough to cut out more cookies.

Remove the cookies from the oven and let them cool completely on the baking sheets, then store in an airtight container in a cool, dry place for up to 2 weeks.

Checkerboard Cookies

MAKES ABOUT 100 COOKIES

With these cookies, no need to decide whether you are in the mood for something chocolaty or something fruity—you get the best of both worlds, since they combine an orange dough and a chocolate dough baked into a beautiful checkerboard pattern. You can freeze the dough, either individually or already assembled as a checkerboard, for up to a month, well wrapped in plastic wrap and stored in an airtight container. You will have several extra egg whites after making this recipe, which you can use for any number of meringue-based recipes in this book, starting with Macarons (page 160). To store extra whites, pour them into a resealable plastic freezer bag, mark the number of whites in the bag, and refrigerate them for up to a week or freeze them for up to a month.

ORANGE DOUGH

10½ tablespoons (150 grams) unsalted butter, at room temperature

½ cup plus ⅓ cup (100 grams) confectioners' sugar

3 large egg yolks

Grated zest from 2 oranges

2⅓ cups (300 grams) all-purpose flour

1 teaspoon (4 grams) salt

CHOCOLATE DOUGH

13 tablespoons (190 grams) unsalted butter, at room temperature

(continued)

MAKE THE ORANGE DOUGH: In the bowl of a stand mixer fitted with the paddle attachment, beat the butter and confectioners' sugar together on low speed until the mixture becomes pale and fluffy. Add the yolks and orange zest and mix until smooth. Add the flour and salt and mix until the dough is just combined.

Remove the dough from the bowl, wrap it in plastic wrap, and refrigerate for about 1 hour, or until it is chilled all the way through.

MAKE THE CHOCOLATE DOUGH: In the bowl of a stand mixer fitted with the paddle attachment, beat the butter and confectioners' sugar together on low speed until the mixture becomes pale and fluffy. Add the yolks and mix until smooth. Add the cocoa powder, flour, and salt and mix until the dough is just combined.

Remove the dough from the bowl, wrap it in plastic wrap, and refrigerate for about 1 hour, or until it is chilled all the way through.

1 cup (125 grams)
confectioners' sugar

4 large egg yolks

⅓ cup (30 grams) Dutch-
process cocoa powder

2½ cups (325 grams)
all-purpose flour

2 teaspoons (8 grams) salt

ASSEMBLE THE COOKIES: Line a baking sheet with parchment or waxed paper.

On a floured surface, roll out the orange dough into a 6-by-10-inch rectangle ½ inch thick. Transfer it to the lined baking sheet and place it in the freezer.

Divide the chocolate dough into two unequal pieces, one-third and two-thirds. Rewrap the one-third in plastic wrap and reserve it in the refrigerator.

On a floured surface, roll out the remaining chocolate dough into a 6-by-10-inch rectangle ½ inch thick. Brush the top of the dough with a little bit of water.

Remove the orange dough from the freezer and place it on top of the chocolate dough, pressing slightly to adhere the two pieces. If the combined dough is soft, return it to the freezer until it firms up again. Otherwise, proceed with the recipe.

With a large chef's knife, cut the dough lengthwise into ½-inch-wide strips (you want an even number of strips). Lay the strips on their sides and trim them to make them even if needed. Take two strips and invert one of them, so one has the orange dough on the left and one has the chocolate dough on the left. Brush the top of one of the strips with water and stack the second strip on top, pressing the two together. You should have a long log of four squares, with the orange and chocolate doughs alternating. Repeat with the remaining strips. You should have about 5 logs. Place the logs back on the lined baking sheet and return them to the freezer. Save the scraps of chocolate dough.

Preheat the oven to 375°F (190°C) and line a baking sheet with parchment paper.

On a floured surface, roll out about half of the reserved chocolate dough along with the chocolate scraps from your trims into a rectangle $\frac{1}{8}$ inch thick, 10 inches wide, and about 12 inches long, so that it is wide and long enough to enrobe two or three checkerboard logs. (You will be covering all the logs with chocolate dough; it is easier to do this in batches, rerolling the scraps as needed.) Trim the edges so that they are straight, reserving the scraps. Make sure that enough flour remains under the dough so that you can lift it carefully without breaking. Try to work quickly so that the dough doesn't warm up too much, or it will be harder to work with.

Brush the first third of the dough with a little water. Remove one of the checkerboard logs from the freezer and place it at one end of the dough. The length of the log should match up with the width of the chocolate dough (10 inches each). Roll the log and the chocolate dough together so that the chocolate dough enrobes it, making sure to press the chocolate dough firmly enough against the log so that the two adhere to each other. Once the log is completely enrobed, trim the chocolate dough where its ends meet, and return the log to the freezer. Repeat until all the logs are enrobed, rolling out the remaining chocolate dough and the scraps into a second 10-inch-wide rectangle as needed to enrobe the remaining logs.

Remove a log from the freezer and cut into $\frac{1}{4}$-inch-thick slices. Place them on the lined baking sheet, and bake for about 8 minutes, or until the cookies just begin to turn a very light brown color.

Remove the cookies from the oven and let them cool completely on the baking sheet. Repeat with the remaining logs. Store the cookies in an airtight container in a cool, dry place for up to 1 week.

Sablés Bretons

MAKES 45 TO 55 COOKIES

Sablés, named for their sandy, buttery texture (sable means "sand"), are popular throughout France, with many regions and towns boasting of their particular, traditional twist. Here, Bretons indicates that they are from Brittany; the trademark of this particular classic cookie is its slight saltiness, since the region is home to the famous Guérande salt marshes, where much great fleur de sel is produced. I bake these thick cookies in a mini muffin pan (metal or silicone) so that they retain their shape. If you bake them without one, on a baking sheet instead, they will spread too much because they don't contain a large amount of flour proportionally to the butter. The sides of the mold contain them and ensure that they have the right thickness, making them a bit denser too. The drop of coffee in the glaze gives it a beautiful color, but is not enough to flavor it.

DOUGH

12 ounces (360 grams) unsalted butter, at room temperature

1¼ cups (240 grams) granulated sugar

4 large egg yolks

3⅓ cups (440 grams) all-purpose flour

1 teaspoon (4 grams) fleur de sel

1 teaspoon (4 grams) baking powder

GLAZE

1 teaspoon (4 grams) instant coffee powder

½ teaspoon (2.5 grams) hot water

1 large egg yolk

MAKE THE DOUGH: In the bowl of a stand mixer fitted with the paddle attachment, beat the butter and sugar until just combined. Add the yolks and mix until smooth, then add the flour, fleur de sel, and baking powder and mix only until just combined. Be careful not to overmix.

Remove the dough from the bowl and wrap it in plastic wrap. Refrigerate for about 30 minutes, or until it is chilled all the way through.

Line a baking sheet with parchment paper.

On a floured surface, roll out the dough to a thickness of ½ inch. Use a 1-inch round cookie cutter to cut it into circles. Place the cookies on the baking sheet and freeze for about 20 minutes, or until firm. This will keep you from tearing into the cookie when crisscrossing it with a fork.

Preheat the oven to 375°F (190°C) and grease two mini muffin pans (if using silicone ones, spray them with nonstick cooking spray).

MAKE THE GLAZE: In a small bowl, whisk together the coffee powder and hot water, then whisk in the egg yolk.

Once the cut cookies are firm, brush the glaze over the tops. With a fork, draw lines across the top of the cookies in a crisscross pattern. Place one cookie, glazed side up, into each cavity of the mini muffin pans. Bake for 10 to 15 minutes, or until the tops are golden brown.

Remove the cookies from the oven and let them cool completely in the pans, then store in an airtight container in a cool, dry place for up to 3 days.

Sablés Nantais

It would be easy to confuse Sablés Nantais and Sablés Bretons (page 43) at first look because they are both round and glazed, but they have differences. This cookie has fluted edges and contains almond flour, and it is flatter. I like it for its crusty, flaky texture. If you want to add another flavor to it, incorporate the grated zest of one lime when you add the egg yolks.

DOUGH

5 tablespoons (75 grams) unsalted butter, softened

⅓ cup plus 2 tablespoons (90 grams) granulated sugar

½ cup (60 grams) almond flour

2 large egg yolks

1⅓ cups plus 2 tablespoons (188 grams) all-purpose flour

Pinch of salt

GLAZE

1 teaspoon (4 grams) instant coffee powder

½ teaspoon (2.5 grams) hot water

1 large egg yolk

MAKE THE DOUGH: In the bowl of a stand mixer fitted with the paddle attachment, beat the butter and sugar together on low speed until the mixture becomes pale and fluffy. Add the almond flour and mix until smooth, then mix in the egg yolks. Add the all-purpose flour and salt and mix until just combined. If the dough has a hard time coming together, you can add 1 to 2 tablespoons (15 to 30 grams) of water at the end.

Remove the dough from the bowl and wrap it in plastic wrap. Refrigerate for about 30 minutes, or until it is chilled all the way through.

Line a baking sheet with parchment paper.

On a floured surface, roll out the dough to a thickness of ⅛ inch. Use a 1-inch round fluted cookie cutter to cut out circles, rerolling the scraps as needed. Place the cookies on the baking sheet, and freeze for about 20 minutes, or until firm. This will keep you from tearing into the cookie when crisscrossing it with a fork.

Preheat the oven to 375°F (190°C).

MAKE THE GLAZE: In a small bowl, whisk together the coffee powder and hot water, then whisk in the egg yolk.

Once the cut cookies are firm, brush the glaze over the tops. With a fork, draw lines across the top of the cookies in a crisscross pattern. Bake for about 8 minutes, or until the tops are a light golden brown color.

Remove the cookies from the oven and let them cool completely on the baking sheet, then store in an airtight container in a cool, dry place for up to 3 days.

> GALETTES AUX NOISETTES, PAGE 29, SABLÉS NANTAIS, PAGE 45, AND SABLÉS AU THÉ, PAGE 49

Sablés au Thé

These small sablés are flavored with Earl Grey tea, but feel free to experiment with your own favorite varieties. Just be aware that some, such as smoked teas, can be overpowering, so you will want to reduce the quantity of tea accordingly, or omit the sprinkling of additional tea over the glaze.

---

3 tablespoons (15 grams) loose Earl Grey tea

8½ tablespoons (120 grams) unsalted butter, at room temperature

5 tablespoons (60 grams) granulated sugar

⅓ cup plus 1 tablespoon (40 grams) almond flour

2 large egg yolks

1¼ cups (160 grams) all-purpose flour

1 teaspoon (4 grams) baking powder

1 teaspoon (4 grams) salt

Grind the tea in a spice grinder until it is finely chopped. It should not turn into a powder. Set aside one-third of the tea.

In the bowl of a stand mixer fitted with the paddle attachment, beat the butter, sugar, and tea together on low speed until the mixture becomes pale and fluffy. Add the almond flour and mix until smooth, then mix in one of the egg yolks. Add the flour, baking powder, and salt and mix until just combined.

Remove the dough from the bowl and wrap it in plastic wrap. Refrigerate for about 30 minutes, or until it is chilled all the way through.

Preheat the oven to 375°F (190°C) and line a baking sheet with parchment paper.

Whisk the remaining egg yolk in a bowl to liquefy it.

On a floured surface, roll out the dough to a thickness of ¼ inch. Use a 1-inch round fluted cookie cutter to cut out circles, rerolling the scraps as necessary. Brush each cookie with the beaten egg yolk, then sprinkle on a small pinch of the reserved tea. Don't overdo it. Place the cookies on the lined baking sheet and bake for 8 to 10 minutes, or until the edges turn a light golden brown color.

Remove the cookies from the oven and let them cool completely on the baking sheet, then store in an airtight container in a cool, dry place for up to 3 days.

Sablés au Chocolat

MAKES ABOUT 30 COOKIES

These sablés have a double dose of chocolate: The dough comprises cocoa powder and chunks of chocolate, which melt when baking and add texture to the cookies when you eat them. Their American name would be chocolate chunk cookies, if I had to pick one. The dark chocolate and cocoa powder make for an intense chocolate flavor; I like serving them when the meal has been rich enough that you might not have room for dessert but still want to finish on a sweet note. They also make elegant gifts, packaged in a small box or gift bag tied with a beautiful ribbon, when you want your guests to go home with a memorable treat.

1 cup plus 1 tablespoon (150 grams) all-purpose flour

¼ cup (25 grams) Dutch-process cocoa powder

1 teaspoon (4 grams) baking powder

1 teaspoon (6 grams) baking soda

1 teaspoon (4 grams) salt

9 tablespoons (130 grams) unsalted butter, at room temperature

3 tablespoons (40 grams) granulated sugar

½ cup (100 grams) light brown sugar

3 tablespoons (45 grams) pure vanilla extract

4 ounces (130 grams) chocolate (70% cacao), chopped into chunks

Preheat the oven to 400°F (200°C) and line a baking sheet with parchment paper.

Over a large bowl, sift together the flour, cocoa powder, baking powder, baking soda, and salt.

In the bowl of a stand mixer fitted with the paddle attachment, beat the butter, granulated sugar, and brown sugar together on low speed until the mixture becomes pale and fluffy. On low speed, slowly add the flour-cocoa mixture, then drizzle in the vanilla and add the chocolate chunks. Mix until everything comes together in a smooth mass.

Divide the dough into thirds and place each on a piece of plastic wrap. Roll each piece of dough into a log 1½ inches in diameter. Twist the ends of each piece of plastic wrap as you would to wrap a candy to help you achieve an evenly round log. Freeze for about 1 hour, or until the logs are chilled all the way through. You can freeze the logs, well wrapped in plastic and stored in an airtight container, for up to 1 month.

You can freeze the logs, well wrapped in plastic and stored in an airtight container, for up to 1 month.

With a sharp knife, cut the dough into ¼-inch-thick slices. Bake for about 8 minutes, just until the cookies are baked enough that you can lift them from the baking sheet without them breaking and they no longer look moist in their center.

Remove the cookies from the oven and transfer them to a cooling rack. Let them cool completely, then store them in an airtight container in a cool, dry place for up to 1 week.

Kipfers

MAKES ABOUT 50 COOKIES

These traditional German cookies take their name from the German word for "croissant," whose crescent shape they share. They are covered in confectioners' sugar, which makes it seem as if they are almost melting in your mouth when you eat them and gives them a festive look perfect for holiday platters. The flavor of this simple cookie is made more complex by almond flour and vanilla extract. The dough is soft, so work with only one-third of it at a time, keeping the rest refrigerated.

14 tablespoons (200 grams) unsalted butter, at room temperature

6 tablespoons (80 grams) granulated sugar

1 cup plus 2 teaspoons (100 grams) almond flour

2 large egg yolks

1 tablespoon (15 grams) pure vanilla extract

2 cups minus 2 tablespoons (250 grams) all-purpose flour

Pinch of salt

2 cups (240 grams) confectioners' sugar

Preheat the oven to 350°F (175°C) and line two baking sheets with parchment paper.

In the bowl of a stand mixer fitted with the paddle attachment, beat the butter and granulated sugar together on low speed until the mixture becomes pale and fluffy. Add the almond flour and mix until combined, then add the egg yolks and vanilla and mix until combined. Add the all-purpose flour and salt and mix until everything just comes together. If the dough is too warm to roll out immediately, remove it from the bowl, wrap it in plastic wrap, and refrigerate for about 30 minutes.

Divide the dough into three batches and keep the remaining dough in the refrigerator, wrapped in plastic, while you work with one batch at a time.

On a floured surface, divide the dough into several pieces and roll it out into strips that are slightly less than ½ inch thick. With a paring knife, cut the dough into pieces about 2½ inches long, about ½ inch wide, and tapered at both ends. Bend the strips into crescent shapes and transfer them to the baking sheets. These cookies can spread, so keep them about 2 inches apart from each other. Bake for about 10 minutes, or until they turn a light golden brown. Remove them from the oven and let them cool completely on the baking sheet or a cooling rack. Repeat with the remaining batches of dough.

Pour the confectioners' sugar into a large bowl and carefully roll each cookie in it until coated. You can also leave the cookies on the baking sheet or cooling rack and heavily sift the confectioners' sugar over them instead. Store them in an airtight container in a cool, dry place for up to 1 week.

Palmiers

MAKES ABOUT 25 COOKIES

Palmiers are a quintessential French cookie. Made with caramelized puff pastry, they are crispy and flaky. When you use store-bought puff pastry, you can prepare a batch in minutes. But if you are looking for an authentic pastry shop–type version, you will find here my quick puff pastry recipe. I encourage you to try it—you will realize that it's not that hard to make your own. You will only need half of the batch for these palmiers, but you can keep the rest in the freezer and use it for any recipe in your repertoire that calls for puff pastry. The finished palmiers log can be frozen, uncooked, before slicing it into cookies.

1 pound (454 grams) puff pastry, thawed

2 cups (400 grams) granulated sugar

Place the puff pastry at the center of a heavily sugared surface, and heavily sprinkle more sugar on top of the dough. Roll out the dough into a ⅛-inch-thick rectangle, continuously adding sugar underneath and on top of the dough while rolling.

Roll the two short edges of the dough toward the center by folding one side over ¼ inch, then doing the same thing on the other side of the rectangle. Continue folding the dough over itself one side at a time. The sides will become thicker as you continue to fold, reaching almost 1 inch on each side. Continue rolling until the two sides meet at the center of the dough, making sure to roll tightly. Fold one side over the other, like closing a book, then place the dough in the freezer for at least 45 minutes, or until it is completely chilled through. You can keep the dough frozen, well wrapped in plastic and stored in an airtight container, for up to 1 month.

Preheat the oven to 400°F (205°C) and line a baking sheet with parchment paper.

Remove the dough from the freezer and cut it into ⅓-inch-thick slices. Place the slices on the baking sheet and sprinkle their tops with a little more sugar. Cover with another sheet of parchment paper, then place a rectangular wire cooling rack on top of the parchment. This will prevent the cookies from puffing up too much.

Bake for 15 to 20 minutes, or until the cookies are a light golden brown color. Be careful: They will go from just the right color to burnt in no time, so keep an eye on them; check for doneness by lifting the edge of the cooling rack and parchment paper. The first time you make them, check the color after about 13 minutes. Once they begin to caramelize, it should only take about 2 more minutes for them to be golden brown. Remove from the oven, remove the cooling rack, and let the cookies cool completely on the baking sheet. Store them in an airtight container in a cool, dry place for up to 1 week.

Quick Puff Pastry

MAKES 2 POUNDS

3½ cups (455 grams) all-purpose flour

2½ teaspoons (10 grams) salt

12 ounces (330 grams) unsalted butter, cold and cut into ½-inch cubes

3 tablespoons plus 1 teaspoon (50 grams) crème fraîche or sour cream

1 cup (240 grams) water

Place the flour and salt in the bowl of a stand mixer fitted with the hook attachment. Beat on low speed for 1 to 2 minutes to combine. Add the butter and crème fraîche or sour cream, and continue beating on low speed. As everything starts to get incorporated, slowly drizzle the water into the bowl with the mixer running. Mix until the dough comes together in a ball.

Transfer the dough to your work surface and, with a sharp knife, slice a ½-inch-deep "X" in the top of the dough. This will help the dough relax. Cut the dough into two equal pieces, wrap each in plastic wrap, and refrigerate for 30 minutes.

On a floured surface, working with one piece of dough at a time, roll out the dough into a 7-by-16-inch rectangle that is ½ inch thick. Use a ruler to measure and to push the dough back into a well-shaped rectangle. This will make your folds even. Arrange the dough with its long side parallel to the edge of the work surface. With a rolling pin, make a top-to-bottom impression in the center of the dough. Brush any excess flour from the surface of the dough (otherwise the dough will not stick to itself, and will create a seam). Fold each side of the dough toward the center, so that the ends almost meet at the crease; there should be a gap of about ¼ inch between the two ends. Brush off any excess flour again, and fold the left side of the dough over the right half, as if you were closing a book. (This process is called a "turn.") Place the dough on a baking sheet, cover with plastic wrap, and refrigerate for 30 minutes.

Place the dough with the long side parallel to the edge of your floured work surface, and again roll out the dough into a 7-by-16-inch rectangle that is ½ inch thick. Make an impression in the center of the dough, and fold each side toward the center so that the ends almost meet at the crease. Brush off any excess flour again, and fold the left side of the dough over the right, as if you were closing a book. (This is the second turn.) Place the dough back on the baking sheet, cover with plastic wrap, and refrigerate for another 30 minutes.

If freezing the dough, do it now. It will keep, tightly wrapped, for up to a month in the freezer. To use, thaw the dough overnight in the refrigerator, then proceed with the third and final turn as follows.

Repeat rolling and folding as above a third time. Refrigerate the dough, covered, for 30 minutes before using. It should be chilled, but the butter should not be too hard. Use as directed in the recipe.

Dipped & Filled Cookies

Cookies that contain chocolate or jam have a slightly extravagant feel. They can act as dessert at the end of a meal, and can be served as an afternoon treat. The Swiss Buttercream Cookies are unique, and not just because they are particularly large as far as cookies go and rarely found in the United States; they also have a strong almond and kirsch flavor, with just enough chocolate to tie it all together. My dad loved a number of cookies that fit this "dipped and filled" category, such as the Bâtons Maréchaux, which are dipped in chocolate and then in nuts, and the Coquilles de Papa, which have a praline filling. Several of the cookies in this chapter can be made with a cookie press if you'd like, such as the Spritz Cookies and the Marguerites, but you can also pipe them instead.

Swiss Buttercream Cookies

MAKES 18 TO 20 COOKIES

One of my former cooks at Payard Pâtisserie, Chris Hereghty, loved making these cookies, which have a nice kirsch flavor and lots of textural contrast. They are typical of Switzerland (kirsch gives that away), so I've honored that heritage in their name. We sell them individually wrapped at François Payard Bakery. They crack when baking, so don't be alarmed when that happens—it is on purpose. The dough is made with almond paste, which gives it chewiness (almost like a soft amaretto cookie). Once baked, the cookies are spread with kirsch buttercream and dipped in chocolate. These are best served on their own rather than as part of an assortment, since eating one is usually enough. (I won't judge you if you eat more, though—they are addictive.) The assembled cookies keep well frozen, so they are great to make ahead. You can simply melt the chocolate, or temper it following the instructions on page 18 for a snappier texture and shinier appearance.

COOKIES

11 ounces (312 grams) almond paste

2¼ cups (270 grams) confectioners' sugar, plus more for dusting

3 large egg whites

BUTTERCREAM

2 large egg whites

½ cup (100 grams) granulated sugar

11 tablespoons (150 grams) unsalted butter, softened but still cold, cut into tablespoons

1 tablespoon (15 grams) kirsch or 1 teaspoon (5 grams) pure vanilla extract

(continued)

MAKE THE COOKIES: Preheat the oven to 375°F (190°C) and line a baking sheet with parchment paper.

In the bowl of a stand mixer fitted with the paddle attachment, beat the almond paste to soften it on medium speed, then add the confectioners' sugar little by little, followed by the egg whites a little at a time as well. Mix until well combined, then carefully scrape the bottom of the bowl to make sure there are no lumps and mix one more time.

With a 1-ounce (2-tablespoon) ice cream scoop, scoop out the dough onto the baking sheet. Dust each cookie generously with confectioners' sugar, then bake for 8 to 10 minutes, or until the edges turn a light golden brown color and the tops have cracked. Remove the cookies from the oven and let them cool completely on the baking sheet.

MAKE THE BUTTERCREAM: Fill a medium pot one-third full with water and bring it to a gentle simmer over medium heat.

5 to 6 ounces (140 to 170 grams) dark chocolate (such as 61% cacao), melted

Place the egg whites and sugar in the bowl of a stand mixer. Reduce the heat to low and place the bowl over the pot, making sure that it is not touching the water. Whisk continuously until the sugar has dissolved and the mixture is hot, 3 to 5 minutes.

Place the bowl in the mixer and beat with the whisk attachment on high speed until the whites hold stiff peaks and are cool, about 5 minutes. Feel the bottom of the bowl to check.

With the motor running, add the softened butter to the meringue, 1 tablespoon at a time. Keep mixing until all of the butter is incorporated and the mixture is light and fluffy. Add the vanilla, if using (if using the kirsch, it will be added later). Transfer the buttercream to a bowl or airtight container, cover, and store at room temperature until ready to use, or in the refrigerator for up to 1 week.

ASSEMBLE THE COOKIES: Turn the cookies upside down on the baking sheet and peel off the parchment paper. With your finger, gently push in the middle of each cookie a little bit to make room for the filling. With a small offset spatula, spread a small amount of buttercream over the bottom of each cookie. Use a pastry brush to brush some kirsch, if using, over the buttercream. Refrigerate for about 30 minutes, until the buttercream has firmed up.

Very gently, pick up each cookie and dip its bottom in melted chocolate, covering the buttercream and about one-third of the cookie. Arrange on the baking sheet and let the chocolate set until completely firm. If a lot of the confectioners' sugar melted during the baking process, you can sprinkle some again over the cookies before serving them. Store them in an airtight container in a cool, dry place for up to 1 week, with a sheet of parchment or waxed paper in between each layer, or in the freezer for up to 1 month. Bring them to room temperature a couple of hours before serving.

Bâtons Maréchaux

MAKES ABOUT 100 COOKIES

These were my dad's favorite cookies because they are so full of flavor and texture, between the almonds inside and the crunch of almonds, sugar, and chocolate that covers them. And of course based on his preferred way to eat cookies, because they are perfect with ice cream. Their name means "marshals' batons," probably because a maréchal de France *receives a baton when being singled out for exceptional military distinction. It's a classic cookie, sometimes made just with almonds, but my dad mixed his with raw sugar for additional crunch in the coating. The cookie dough itself also contains almonds. You can coat them with dark or milk chocolate.*

⅔ cup (60 grams) sliced almonds

5 tablespoons (60 grams) plus ¼ cup (50 grams) granulated sugar

3 large egg whites

1 teaspoon (4 grams) cream of tartar or 2 teaspoons (10 grams) freshly squeezed lemon juice

1 tablespoon (10 grams) all-purpose flour

1 cup (140 grams) coarsely chopped almonds

½ cup (100 grams) turbinado sugar, such as Sugar in the Raw

8 ounces (240 grams) chocolate, melted

Preheat the oven to 400°F (200°C) and line two baking sheets with parchment paper.

In a food processor, mix the sliced almonds with 5 tablespoons (60 grams) of the granulated sugar.

Place the egg whites and cream of tartar or lemon juice in the bowl of a stand mixer fitted with the whisk attachment, and whisk on medium speed until medium to firm peaks form. Slowly sprinkle the remaining ¼ cup (50 grams) granulated sugar over the egg whites and continue whisking until they form stiff peaks. (To ensure you have reached stiff peaks, stop the mixer and lift the whisk from the bowl; if the peaks that form stay pointed, the whites are ready.) Remove the bowl from the mixer and, with a silicone spatula, fold in the flour and the almond-sugar mixture.

Transfer the mixture to a pastry bag fitted with a ¼-inch round pastry tip. You can also just cut a ¼-inch opening into the tip of the pastry bag.

Pipe the mixture onto the lined baking sheets in 3-inch strips, not pressing down too much so that the cookies stay as close to ¼ inch wide as possible. They will spread a bit when baking. Sprinkle the tops with the chopped almonds and turbinado sugar. Bake for about 12 minutes, or until the cookies turn a light golden brown color.

Remove the cookies from the oven and let them cool completely on the baking sheet. Turn them upside down so that the almonds are on the bottom, and with a small offset spatula or a spoon, spread a thin layer of melted chocolate onto the backs of the cookies. Leave them on the baking sheet in a cool, dry place until the chocolate is completely firm, about 30 minutes. Store in an airtight container in a cool, dry place for up to 1 week, with a sheet of parchment or waxed paper in between each layer.

Spritz Cookies

MAKES ABOUT 40 SANDWICH COOKIES

Spritz cookies are among the most classic types of butter cookies, with a simple, crumbly dough that is typically piped or pushed through a cookie press. They can be sandwiched, dipped, or topped with nuts or colorful sprinkles. Here I do a bit of it all: a smooth ganache filling, a dip in melted chocolate, and crunchy nuts as garnish. The ganache can be flavored with a teaspoon (5 grams) of pure mint or orange extract, or you can use jam instead. The dough is very stiff, so it's best to use a cloth pastry bag, not a plastic one, so that it doesn't burst when you pipe the cookies. A cookie press makes it easier to handle the stiff dough, but it will make for wider cookies, and fewer of them.

DOUGH

8 tablespoons (120 grams) unsalted butter, at room temperature

½ cup (110 grams) light brown sugar

1 large egg

1 teaspoon (5 grams) pure vanilla extract

2¼ cups (290 grams) all-purpose flour

¼ teaspoon (1 gram) salt

FILLING

1 cup (190 grams) semisweet chocolate chips

3 tablespoons (45 grams) milk

1 cup (120 grams) confectioners' sugar

(continued)

MAKE THE COOKIES: Preheat the oven to 375°F (190°C) and line a baking sheet with parchment paper.

In the bowl of a stand mixer fitted with the paddle attachment, beat the butter and brown sugar together on low speed until the mixture becomes pale and fluffy. Add the egg and the vanilla and mix until well combined, then add the flour and salt and mix until just combined.

With a spatula, transfer the dough to a pastry bag fitted with a 1-inch star pastry tip. Pipe the cookies into 1-inch-wide, 3-inch-long strips. If using a cookie press, fit it with the disk that has a dented rectangle opening; those will spread more. Press the dough into long strips that run the length of the baking sheet. Bake for 8 to 10 minutes, or until the edges of the cookies just begin to slightly brown. Remove from the oven and immediately cut the long strips into 3-inch pieces. Let them cool completely on the baking sheet. They will keep in an airtight container in a cool, dry place for up to 1 week.

MAKE THE FILLING: Fill a medium pot one-third full with water and bring it to a gentle simmer over medium heat. Place the chocolate chips and milk in a large bowl that will fit over the pot

ASSEMBLY

1 cup (130 grams) mixed nuts, such as pecans, walnuts, and pistachios, toasted (see page 21) and chopped

without touching the water. Reduce the heat to low and place the bowl over the pot. Melt the chocolate, stirring gently once or twice. Remove from the heat and whisk in the confectioners' sugar until the mixture is smooth.

ASSEMBLE THE COOKIES: Once cooled, invert half of the cookies and spread a small amount of filling onto the bottom of each. Place another cookie of similar size over the filling, and press lightly to sandwich them. Dip both ends of the cookies into the chocolate filling, and then dip into the chopped nuts. If the chocolate hardens during the process, put it back over the simmering water until it melts again. Let the dipped parts of the cookies firm up, 15 to 30 minutes, then store in an airtight container in a cool, dry place for up to 1 week, with a sheet of parchment or waxed paper in between each layer, or in the freezer for up to 1 month.

B&B with Praline

MAKES ABOUT 50 SANDWICH COOKIES

This dough is very liquid; coating the baking sheet with softened butter and flour prevents the batter from spreading too much and helps the cookies retain their shape as they bake. If desired, dip the cookies halfway into melted dark or milk chocolate after filling them, as in the Aidas on page 73. Avoid white chocolate, which, paired with the already sweet praline filling, would make the cookies too cloying.

4 tablespoons (120 grams) unsalted butter, softened

½ cup (60 grams) all-purpose flour

1 cup plus 2 tablespoons (150 grams) hazelnut flour

¾ cup (150 grams) granulated sugar

5 large egg whites

3 tablespoons (50 grams) unsalted butter, melted

1½ teaspoons (7 grams) pure vanilla extract

¼ cup (75 grams) praline paste

Preheat the oven to 400°F (200°C) and line two baking sheets with parchment paper. With a pastry brush, paint the parchment paper with the softened butter, then dust with ¼ cup (30 grams) of the all-purpose flour. Shake the pans to remove any excess flour.

In a food processor, grind together the hazelnut flour and sugar until combined. Be careful not to let the mixture turn into a paste. Transfer to a large bowl, then, with a silicone spatula, stir in the remaining ¼ cup (30 grams) all-purpose flour and the egg whites. Stir in the melted butter and vanilla.

With a spatula, transfer the mixture to a pastry bag fitted with a ½-inch pastry tip. You can also just cut a ½-inch opening into the tip of the pastry bag. Pipe the cookies onto the prepared baking sheets in 1-inch circles, and tap or drop the pans from a height of a few inches to slightly flatten the cookies. Bake for 8 to 10 minutes, or until the edges turn a light golden brown color but the centers are still white. Remove the cookies from the oven and let them cool completely on the baking sheets.

Once cool, invert half of the cookies and spread a small amount of praline paste onto the bottom of each. Place another cookie of similar size over the praline paste, and press lightly to sandwich them, then store them in an airtight container in a cool, dry place for up to 3 days.

Aidas

MAKES 100 SANDWICH COOKIES

These cookies are small but rich: Their dough contains almond paste and chocolate, and they are filled with praline paste and dipped in more chocolate. It makes them perfect to serve instead of a full-size dessert. This is one of my dad's recipes; but while he only filled them, I dip them too, which allows them to stand on one end. This recipe makes a large amount of cookies and the dough softens up quickly when you roll it out, so unless you need a lot of cookies, I suggest you bake half of it at a time, reducing the amount of filling accordingly.

DOUGH

2 ounces (56 grams, about 3½ tablespoons) almond paste

½ cup (60 grams) confectioners' sugar

15 tablespoons (220 grams) unsalted butter, at room temperature

2 ounces (56 grams) chocolate (61% cacao), melted

2½ cups (320 grams) all-purpose flour

3 large egg whites

Pinch of salt

ASSEMBLY

¼ cup (75 grams) praline paste

8 ounces (240 grams) chocolate, melted

MAKE THE DOUGH: In the bowl of a stand mixer fitted with the paddle attachment, beat the almond paste and confectioners' sugar together on medium speed until the mixture becomes pale and fluffy. Add the butter a little at a time to keep lumps from forming, then mix in the melted chocolate until everything is combined. On low speed, starting with the flour, alternate adding the flour and egg whites (this will ensure that the mixture stays smooth). Add the salt and mix until fully combined.

Remove the dough from the bowl, divide it in half, wrap each half in plastic wrap, and refrigerate for about 2 hours, or until it is chilled all the way through. You can also freeze the dough, well wrapped in plastic and stored in an airtight container, for up to 1 month.

On a lightly floured surface, working with one piece of dough at a time, roll out the dough until it is about ⅛ inch thick. Transfer it to a parchment-lined tray or baking sheet, and place it back in the freezer until it firms up again, about 30 minutes.

Preheat the oven to 350°F (180°C) and line two baking sheets with parchment paper.

Use a 1¼-inch round cookie cutter to cut out circles and transfer them to the baking sheets. Bake for 10 to 12 minutes, or until the edges turn a light brown color. Remove the cookies from the oven and let them cool completely on the baking sheets. Repeat with the remaining dough.

ASSEMBLE THE COOKIES: Invert half of the cookies and spread a small amount of praline paste onto the bottom of each. Place another cookie of similar size over the praline paste, and press lightly to sandwich them. Dip the sandwiched cookies halfway into the melted chocolate. To let the chocolate dry, you can stand the cookie up on its tip or lay it down. Refrigerate until the chocolate is cold and firm, about 30 minutes, then store the cookies in an airtight container in a cool, dry place for up to 3 days, with a sheet of parchment or waxed paper in between each layer.

Peanut Butter Biarritz Cookies

MAKES ABOUT 100 SANDWICH COOKIES

In France, these would more traditionally be made with praline paste, but I like peanut butter and have grown fond of this slightly Americanized version. If you make the cookies ahead of time, wait until you are ready to serve them to spread them with peanut butter. Otherwise the moisture in the filling will make them lose their crunchiness.

1 cup (100 grams) hazelnut flour

½ cup (100 grams) plus 2 tablespoons (25 grams) granulated sugar

½ cup plus 2 tablespoons (80 grams) all-purpose flour, sifted

⅓ cup plus 4 teaspoons (100 grams) milk

Grated zest of 1 orange

5 large egg whites

5 tablespoons plus 1 teaspoon (80 grams) unsalted butter, melted and kept warm

½ cup (125 grams) smooth peanut butter

Preheat the oven to 400°F (200°C), line two baking sheets with parchment paper, spray them with nonstick cooking spray, and dust them very lightly with flour.

In a food processor, grind together the hazelnut flour and ½ cup (100 grams) of the sugar until combined. Transfer to a large bowl, then, with a silicone spatula, stir in the all-purpose flour, milk, and orange zest.

Place the egg whites in the bowl of a stand mixer fitted with the whisk attachment, and whisk at medium speed until medium to firm peaks form. Slowly sprinkle the remaining 2 tablespoons (25 grams) sugar over the egg whites and continue whisking until they form stiff peaks. Remove the bowl from the mixer and, with a silicone spatula, fold the whipped whites into the hazelnut mixture, then fold in the melted butter until fully combined.

With a spatula, transfer the dough to a pastry bag fitted with a ½-inch pastry tip. Pipe the cookies onto the prepared baking sheets in 1-inch circles. Bake for 8 to 10 minutes, or until they turn a light golden brown color. Remove the cookies from the oven and let them cool completely on the baking sheets. They will keep in an airtight container in a cool, dry place for up to 1 week.

Invert half of the cookies and spread a small amount of peanut butter onto the bottom of each. Place another cookie over the peanut butter, and press lightly to sandwich them. Serve immediately.

Coquilles de Papa

MAKES ABOUT 40 SANDWICH COOKIES

My dad baked a lot of cookies for his pastry shops in Nice, France. So I like to make some of his favorites and think of our times together, when I'd bake alongside him or we'd sit together and enjoy a few cookies with a cup of coffee. These, with meringue-based shells and a praline paste filling, were ones he made often; you first bite into the crispy shells and then get to the rich and soft praline—a delight. You will find praline paste in gourmet shops or online (see Resources, page 266), or see page 22 for a recipe.

½ cup (60 grams) hazelnut flour

⅓ cup (60 grams) plus ¼ cup (50 grams) granulated sugar

3 large egg whites

1 teaspoon (4 grams) cream of tartar or 2 teaspoons (10 grams) freshly squeezed lemon juice

1 tablespoon (10 grams) all-purpose flour

¼ cup (75 grams) praline paste

Preheat the oven to 400°F (200°C), line two baking sheets with parchment paper, spray them with nonstick cooking spray, and dust them very lightly with flour.

In a food processor, grind together the hazelnut flour and ⅓ cup (60 grams) of the sugar until combined. Be careful not to let the mixture turn into a paste.

Place the egg whites and cream of tartar or lemon juice in the bowl of a stand mixer fitted with the whisk attachment, and whisk on medium speed until medium to firm peaks form. Slowly sprinkle the remaining ¼ cup (50 grams) sugar over the egg whites and continue whisking until they form stiff peaks. Remove the bowl from the mixer and, with a silicone spatula, fold in the all-purpose flour and the hazelnut-sugar mixture.

With a spatula, transfer the dough to a pastry bag fitted with a 1-inch star pastry tip. Hold the bag at a 45-degree angle, and pipe the cookies into a shell shape. Bake for 8 to 10 minutes, or until they turn a light golden brown color. Remove the cookies from the oven and let them cool completely on the baking sheets.

Once cool, invert half of the cookies and spread a small amount of praline paste onto the bottom of each. Place another cookie of similar size over the praline paste, and press lightly to sandwich them, then store them in an airtight container in a cool, dry place for up to 3 days.

Duchesses

These classic cookies are sophisticated and elegant—but the crisp rice cereal adds a more whimsical touch. When I was growing up, they were a fixture in my dad's rotation of cookies, and I loved grabbing one (or maybe two) on my way home from school. Because of their meringue base, they have a very different texture than typical butter-and-flour cookies. They are easy to make in large quantities and stand storage very well. Praline paste is composed of hazelnuts and/or almonds and sugar; it is available through a variety of sources online (or see page 22 for a recipe). You can use smooth peanut butter if you prefer, but the taste will be very different.

COOKIES

1¾ cups (175 grams) almond flour

½ cup plus ⅓ cup (100 grams) confectioners' sugar

1 tablespoon plus 2 teaspoons (25 grams) unsalted butter, melted

4 large egg whites

1 teaspoon (4 grams) cream of tartar or 2 teaspoons (10 grams) freshly squeezed lemon juice

⅓ cup plus 1 tablespoon (75 grams) granulated sugar

¼ cup (40 grams) finely chopped almonds

(continued)

MAKE THE COOKIES: Preheat the oven to 375°F (190°C) and line a baking sheet with parchment paper.

Sift together the almond flour and confectioners' sugar over a bowl. Stir in the melted butter.

Place the egg whites and cream of tartar or lemon juice in the bowl of a stand mixer fitted with the whisk attachment, and whisk on high speed. When the whites begin to form medium to firm peaks, gradually sprinkle the granulated sugar over them. Continue whisking until the whites form stiff peaks. (To ensure you have reached stiff peaks, stop the mixer and lift the whisk from the bowl; if the peaks that form stay pointed, the whites are ready.)

Remove the bowl from the mixer and stir a large dollop of the egg whites into the almond mixture to lighten it up. Fold the lightened mixture into the egg whites with a silicone spatula.

With a spatula, transfer the mixture to a pastry bag fitted with a ¼-inch star pastry tip. Pipe the mixture onto the lined baking sheet in 2-inch strips. Sprinkle the top of each cookie with the chopped almonds and immediately bake for 8 to 10 minutes, or until they turn a slightly light golden brown color.

ASSEMBLY

½ cup (150 grams) praline paste

½ cup (20 grams) crisp rice cereal

8 ounces (227 grams) chocolate, melted

Remove the cookies from the oven and let them cool completely on the baking sheet or a cooling rack. When the cookies are cool, match them in pairs that are as close in size as possible, to make for even sandwiches.

ASSEMBLE THE COOKIES: In a medium bowl, combine the praline paste and ¼ cup (10 grams) of the rice cereal. Place the remaining ¼ cup cereal in a small bowl and the melted chocolate in a third bowl. Place a wire cooling rack on a baking sheet (the one you just used is fine) near the bowls.

Use a spoon or small offset spatula to spread a thin layer of the praline mixture on the bottom of one cookie. Top with another cookie to create a sandwich. Hold the sandwiched cookie by one end and dip it about halfway down its length into the melted chocolate, then into the remaining rice cereal. Place the sandwich on the cooling rack, and repeat the process with the remaining cookies until all are made into sandwiches. Let the chocolate garnish firm up for about 30 minutes. Store the finished cookies in an airtight container in a cool, dry place for up to 2 days.

French-Style Oreos

My version of Oreos, probably the most beloved American cookie after chocolate chips, does not include a filling. Instead, I drizzle melted white chocolate over the cocoa cookies. I find that this makes them a little less sweet and more grown up than the original. But feel free to sandwich two of those with a bit of white chocolate ganache—or any of your favorite ganaches—to send them over the top. That should make them a veritable hit at a children's birthday party, for example.

½ cup plus 1 tablespoon (75 grams) all-purpose flour

¾ cup (75 grams) Dutch-process cocoa powder

1 teaspoon (6 grams) baking soda

1 teaspoon (3 grams) ground cinnamon

7 tablespoons (100 grams) unsalted butter, at room temperature

⅓ cup plus 1 tablespoon (80 grams) light brown sugar

⅓ cup (80 grams) granulated sugar

2 large egg whites

1 teaspoon (5 grams) pure vanilla extract

3⅓ cups (100 grams) crisp rice cereal

8 ounces (240 grams) white chocolate, melted (see page 17)

Preheat the oven to 350°F (180°C) and line two baking sheets with parchment paper.

Over a large bowl, sift together the flour, cocoa, baking soda, and cinnamon.

In the bowl of a stand mixer fitted with the paddle attachment, beat the butter, brown sugar, and granulated sugar together on low speed until the mixture becomes pale and fluffy. Add the egg whites and vanilla and mix until smooth and homogeneous, then add the flour and cocoa mixture and mix until just combined. Add the rice cereal and mix until it is evenly incorporated into the dough.

With a tablespoon, spoon the dough onto the baking sheets. Bake for 8 to 10 minutes, or until the cookies start to firm up around the edges and are no longer wet at the center. Remove the cookies from the oven and let them cool completely on the baking sheet or on a cooling rack.

Once cool, dip a fork or a spoon in the melted white chocolate, then drizzle the chocolate over the cookies in a zigzag or straight line pattern, depending on your preference. Allow the chocolate to set, which will take 1 hour at room temperature, then store the cookies in an airtight container in a cool, dry place for up to 4 days, placing a sheet of parchment or waxed paper in between each layer.

Rosaces au Chocolat

MAKES ABOUT 25 SANDWICH COOKIES

These cookies feature a lightly orange-flavored chocolate dough piped into an elegant rosette shape that might even resemble an orange, sandwiched with a ganache filling. The ganache will make more than you need for the cookies, but it will keep in the refrigerator for about a week. Use it to sandwich other cookies, such as two small sablés, for example. Make the ganache before you start the cookies, so that it has time to set up and reach a pipable consistency by the time the cookies are baked and cooled. Because the dough is firm, it is best to pipe it using a fabric pastry bag, since a plastic one might burst. When piping, squeeze the dough just above the pastry tip, which gives you more control over a thick and heavy dough like this one, doesn't strain your hands as much, and helps keep the bag from bursting. You can also use a larger star tip, making the cookies a little bigger, if you have difficulty piping.

GANACHE

10 ounces (300 grams) chocolate (60% cacao), finely chopped

1¼ cups (300 grams) heavy cream

COOKIES

8 ounces plus 1 tablespoon (240 grams) unsalted butter, at room temperature

½ cup (100 grams) granulated sugar

Grated zest of 1 orange

2 large eggs

2½ cups plus 2 tablespoons (350 grams) all-purpose flour

¼ cup (25 grams) Dutch-process cocoa powder

MAKE THE GANACHE: Place the chocolate in a small bowl.

In a small pan, heat the cream until it just begins to simmer. Pour the hot cream over the chocolate and begin to slowly whisk, starting in the center of the bowl and working your way out to the edges. Continue whisking until the chocolate is fully melted and the ganache is glossy.

Cover the bowl with plastic wrap and refrigerate until the ganache sets to a thick, pipable consistency, at least 1 hour, stirring occasionally. You can prepare the ganache up to 1 week ahead. When ready to use, transfer it to a pastry bag and make a ¼-inch cut in its tip, or use directly from the bowl.

MAKE THE COOKIES: Preheat the oven to 375°F (190°C) and line a baking sheet with parchment paper.

In the bowl of a stand mixer fitted with the paddle attachment, beat the butter, sugar, and orange zest together on low speed until the mixture becomes pale and fluffy. Add the eggs and mix until fully combined. Add the flour and cocoa powder and mix until well combined.

MAKE THE GANACHE: Place the chocolate in a small bowl.

In a small pan, heat the cream until it just begins to simmer. Pour the hot cream over the chocolate and begin to slowly whisk, starting in the center of the bowl and working your way out to the edges. Continue whisking until the chocolate is fully melted and the ganache is glossy.

Cover the bowl with plastic wrap and refrigerate until the ganache sets to a thick, pipable consistency, at least 1 hour, stirring occasionally. You can prepare the ganache up to 1 week ahead. When ready to use, transfer it to a pastry bag and make a ¼-inch cut in its tip, or use directly from the bowl.

MAKE THE COOKIES: Preheat the oven to 375°F (190°C) and line a baking sheet with parchment paper.

In the bowl of a stand mixer fitted with the paddle attachment, beat the butter, sugar, and orange zest together on low speed until the mixture becomes pale and fluffy. Add the eggs and mix until fully combined. Add the flour and cocoa powder and mix until well combined.

Raspberry Lunettes

MAKES ABOUT 50 SANDWICH COOKIES

The name of these cookies translates to "eyeglasses," because of their oval shape with two round cutouts. Splitting the dough in half before rolling it makes it easier to roll and cut. Since half of the cookies have cutouts and half do not, you will need to bake them on separate baking sheets to avoid under- or overbaking them. Adding water to the dough means that it won't shrink much and will perfectly retain the shape into which it is cut, which is important for this particular cookie.

8 ounces (240 grams) unsalted butter, at room temperature

1¼ cups (240 grams) granulated sugar

2 large eggs

3¼ cups (480 grams) all-purpose flour

1¾ cups (120 grams) almond flour

1 tablespoon (15 grams) water

2 cups (600 grams) raspberry jam

½ cup (60 grams) confectioners' sugar

In the bowl of a stand mixer fitted with the paddle attachment, beat the butter and granulated sugar together on low speed until the mixture becomes pale and fluffy. Add the eggs and mix until everything is fully combined. Add the all-purpose flour and almond flour and mix until fully combined, then add the water and mix until smooth.

Remove the dough from the bowl, divide it in half, wrap each half in plastic wrap, and refrigerate for about 2 hours, or until it is chilled all the way through.

Preheat the oven to 375°F (190°C) and line two baking sheets with parchment paper.

Take out half of the dough from the refrigerator. On a lightly floured surface, roll out the dough until it is ¼ inch thick. With a 2-inch tapered oval cookie cutter, cut out the dough and place the ovals on a baking sheet. Repeat with the rest of the dough from the refrigerator, rerolling the scraps as necessary.

Using a small round cookie cutter or a pastry tip, cut two small circles out of half of the cookies (place the cookies with the cutouts all on one baking sheet), to create an eyeglasses-like shape as pictured. Bake for 8 to 10 minutes, or until they just begin to turn a light golden brown. The cookies with cutouts will bake slightly faster than the ones without. Remove the cookies from the oven and let them cool completely on the baking sheets.

Invert the whole cookies and spread a small amount of jam onto the bottom of each. Dust the cutout cookies with confectioners' sugar, and place one on each of the cookies with jam. Press lightly to sandwich them, then store them in an airtight container in a cool, dry place for up to 1 week.

Marguerites

MAKES ABOUT 50 COOKIES

Marguerites take their name from their daisy-like shape (marguerite in French), accentuated by a bright jam filling in the center. At Payard, I use a bake-proof raspberry jam, which is slightly thicker and doesn't run when baked. It can be hard to find outside of commercial distribution, so you can either slightly cook your jam on the stove to thicken it or, more easily, pipe and bake the cookies unfilled and add the jam after the cookies have cooled.

7 tablespoons (100 grams) unsalted butter, at room temperature

½ cup plus ⅓ cup (100 grams) confectioners' sugar, plus more for dusting

Grated zest of 1 lemon

Grated zest of 1 orange

¼ teaspoon (1 gram) salt

4 large egg whites

1¾ cups plus 1 tablespoon (240 grams) all-purpose flour

1 tablespoon plus 2 teaspoons (20 grams) baking powder

⅓ cup (100 grams) raspberry jam, preferably bake-proof (see note, above)

Preheat the oven to 350°F (180°C) and line a baking sheet with parchment paper.

In the bowl of a stand mixer fitted with the paddle attachment, beat the butter, confectioners' sugar, lemon and orange zests, and salt together on low speed until the mixture becomes pale and fluffy. Add the egg whites one by one, waiting until each is fully incorporated before adding the next one, and mix until everything is fully combined. Add in the flour and baking powder, mixing until just combined.

Transfer the dough to a pastry bag fitted with a 1-inch star pastry tip (if you have one, use a daisy-shaped tip). Hold the bag vertically and keep the tip pressed onto the pan, without raising it. Squeeze the bag and the dough will press out of the side cuts of the tip, creating a daisy shape. Wet your thumb or the back of a small melon baller, and depress a well in the center of each cookie. Do not go all the way through, but make it deep and wide enough to contain the jam. Pipe or spoon a small amount of jam into the center of each cookie. Bake for 10 to 15 minutes, or until the edges turn a light golden brown color.

Remove the cookies from the oven and transfer them to a cooling rack. Let them cool completely, then store them in an airtight container in a cool, dry place for up to 1 week, placing a sheet of parchment or waxed paper in between each layer.

Apple Compote Cookies

MAKES ABOUT 50 COOKIES

These cookies resemble Marguerites (page 89), but with an almond dough and apple compote instead of raspberry jam. You can use other types of compotes if you'd like, to take advantage of fruits throughout the seasons. They are delicious with a nectarine or peach compote in the summer, for example, as you might find at your farmers' market. The key is for the compote not to be too runny; if yours is too liquid, set it to drain in a strainer lined with cheesecloth for about an hour, until the excess liquid has run out. You'll need about 1¼ cups of compote total, using about 1 teaspoon per cookie.

⅔ cup plus ¼ cup (85 grams) almond flour

1½ cups (195 grams) all-purpose flour

14 tablespoons (170 grams) unsalted butter, at room temperature

¼ cup plus 1 teaspoon (55 grams) granulated sugar

3 large egg whites

1 teaspoon (5 grams) pure vanilla extract

1 jar apple compote

Preheat the oven to 350°F (180°C) and line a baking sheet with parchment paper.

In a small bowl, whisk together the almond flour and all-purpose flour to combine them.

In the bowl of a stand mixer fitted with the paddle attachment, beat the butter and sugar together on low speed until the mixture becomes pale and fluffy. Add one-third of the almond-flour mixture and one of the egg whites, mixing until well combined. Repeat with the remaining flour mixture and egg whites, in two more additions, until everything is combined, then stir in the vanilla.

With a spatula, transfer the mixture to a pastry bag fitted with a 1-inch star pastry tip (if you have one, use a daisy-shaped tip). Hold the bag vertically and keep the tip pressed onto the pan, without raising it. Squeeze the bag and the dough will press out of the side cuts of the tip, creating a daisy shape. Wet your thumb or the back of a small melon baller, and depress a well in the center of the cookie. Do not go all the way through, but make it deep and wide enough to contain the compote. Bake for 10 to 12 minutes, or until the edges turn a light golden brown color.

Remove the cookies from the oven and let them cool completely. Once cool, pipe or spoon a small amount of the compote into the center of each cookie, then store them in an airtight container in a cool, dry place for up to 3 days, placing a sheet of parchment or waxed paper in between each layer.

Apricot Linzer Hearts

MAKES 25 TO 30 SANDWICH COOKIES

Linzer cookies consist of a hazelnut dough topped with jam and are individually sized variations of a linzer torte, which usually has a beautiful lattice top over the jam. The jam of choice is traditionally raspberry, but I like to give it a twist with apricot jam, or sometimes with fig jam as well; you should feel free to do the same and use your favorite. The number of cookies you'll get with this recipe depends on how large a cookie cutter you use. With a 2-inch cutter, you'll have about 25 sandwich cookies. If you like a strong cinnamon taste, you can add up to 1 tablespoon (8 grams) total to the dough. This dough warms up quickly when out of the refrigerator, so work with it in two batches. On the baking sheets, arrange the cookies head to tail to fit as many as possible. Keep all of the cookies with cutouts on the same baking sheet, since they will bake for a different amount of time than the ones that are left whole.

---

16 tablespoons (240 grams) unsalted butter, at room temperature

½ cup (100 grams) granulated sugar

1¼ cups (100 grams) hazelnut flour

¾ cup (100 grams) all-purpose flour

1½ teaspoons (5 grams) ground cinnamon

Pinch of salt

1 large egg yolk

1 cup (300 grams) apricot jam

¼ cup (30 grams) confectioners' sugar

In the bowl of a stand mixer fitted with the paddle attachment, beat the butter, granulated sugar, hazelnut flour, all-purpose flour, cinnamon, and salt together on low speed until the mixture becomes homogeneous. Add the egg yolk and mix until everything is fully combined.

Remove the dough from the bowl, divide it in half, wrap each half in plastic wrap, and refrigerate for at least 2 hours, until it is chilled all the way through.

Line two baking sheets with parchment paper.

Take out half of the dough from the refrigerator. On a generously floured surface, roll it out until it is ¼ inch thick. With a 1- or 2-inch heart-shaped cookie cutter, cut out the dough and place the hearts on a baking sheet. Repeat with the rest of the dough from the refrigerator, rerolling the scraps as well. Using a smaller heart-shaped cookie cutter, cut out the centers of half of the cookies (place the cookies with the cutouts all on the same baking sheet, so that they bake evenly). Return the baking sheets to the refrigerator for 2 more hours.

Preheat the oven to 340°F (170°C).

Bake for 8 to 10 minutes, or until the cookies just begin to turn a light golden brown. The cookies with the cutouts will bake slightly faster than the ones without. Remove the cookies from the oven and let them cool completely on the baking sheets.

Invert the whole cookies and spread a small amount of jam onto the bottom of each. Dust the cutout cookies with confectioners' sugar, and place one on each of the cookies with jam. Press lightly to sandwich them, then store them in an airtight container in a cool, dry place for up to 3 days, placing a sheet of parchment or waxed paper in between each layer.

Nutty, Spiced & Fruity Cookies

As I've mentioned, a lot of French cookies include almond flour; that is true of the *gommés* in this chapter, which have a chewy texture. But I also like using other nuts, whether in whole or ground forms, from pistachios to coconut. Pecans are not common in France, where we more typically use walnuts, but as a nod to my American customers, I make Pecan Squares, my take on pecan pie. In the fall especially, I like to pair nutty and spiced cookies in an assortment, since both go well with warm cider or hot chocolate. In addition to the always classic cinnamon, I use a lot of five-spice and cardamom—those spices have deep, complex flavors. As for fruits, the recipes in this chapter are not about fresh fruits or jams; rather, they all employ candied and dried fruits. It means that they both transcend seasons and are perfect for a holiday table as alternatives to fruitcakes or plum puddings. A number of these cookies, such as Pain Turc and Cinnamon Cookies, are of the slice-and-bake variety, so you can prepare the dough ahead of time and keep it in the freezer until ready to bake.

Coconut Rochers

MAKES ABOUT 50 COOKIES

I like shaping these rochers like pyramids, but since rocher is the French word for "rock" or "boulder", you can really think of them as boulders, too, and shape them into balls instead. For some variety, you can fold in finely chopped chocolate chips or dried fruit when you add the coconut, or dip the cookies halfway into melted chocolate. When shaping the cookies, it's easier to shape them all into balls first, arrange them on the baking sheet, and then pinch them all into pyramids.

---

5 large egg whites

¾ cup (150 grams) granulated sugar

3¾ cups (250 grams) unsweetened desiccated coconut

Pinch of salt

Preheat the oven to 425°F (220°C) and line a baking sheet with parchment paper.

Fill a medium pot one-third full with water and bring it to a gentle simmer over medium heat.

Place the egg whites and sugar in the bowl of a stand mixer. Reduce the heat to low and place the bowl over the pot, making sure the bottom is not touching the water. Whisk continuously until the sugar has dissolved and the mixture is hot, 3 to 5 minutes. Do not overheat or the eggs will cook.

Place the bowl on the mixer and, using the whisk attachment, beat on high speed until the whites hold stiff peaks and are cool, about 5 minutes. Feel the bottom of the bowl to check. Remove the bowl from the mixer and, with a silicone spatula, fold in the coconut and salt.

Dip your fingers in water so that the dough does not stick to them, then take approximately a tablespoon amount of dough and roll it into a ball in your hands. With your fingertips, taper and pinch the top of the ball to form it into a pyramid. Leave the tips somewhat flat, as pictured, or they might darken too much in the oven. Bake for about 10 minutes, or until a crust forms on the outside of the cookie and the center remains moist. Remove the cookies from the oven and let them cool completely on the baking sheet, then store them in an airtight container in a cool, dry place for 3 to 4 days.

Granola Cookies

MAKES ABOUT 40 COOKIES

I sell these bar cookies at my store in Las Vegas. We always have them available there, since people like to grab one as a snack. They are sweet, but because they are made with granola they can almost pass for breakfast in a place like Vegas. If you prefer, feel free to coat the cookies in milk or dark chocolate instead of white. Be careful not to overcook them; since they contain a large amount of sugar, they will hold their heat and continue to caramelize after you remove them from the oven. If they overcook, they will end up very tough and chewy. If you like thicker granola cookies, double the recipe, or bake the same amount in a smaller dish, such as a 9-inch square baking dish or a 9-inch round cake pan.

---

14 tablespoons (200 grams) unsalted butter

6 tablespoons (120 grams) honey

¼ cup (60 grams) water

3 cups (300 grams) rolled oats

1¼ cups (100 grams) sliced almonds

1 cup (110 grams) walnuts, chopped

⅔ cup (100 grams) raisins

3⅓ cups (400 grams) confectioners' sugar

⅔ cup (80 grams) all-purpose flour

8 ounces (240 grams) white chocolate, melted

Preheat the oven to 325°F (160°C). Spray a 9-by-13-inch glass baking dish with nonstick cooking spray, line it with parchment paper, and spray it again.

In a small pot, combine the butter, honey, and the water over low heat, stirring a couple of times to ensure that the butter and honey melt evenly without burning.

In a large bowl, stir together the oats, almonds, walnuts, raisins, confectioners' sugar, and flour. Once the butter and honey mixture is completely melted and hot, pour it over the granola mixture and stir until fully combined. Work fast; the dough will set quickly. Pour the dough into the prepared dish and spread it out evenly with an offset spatula. If the dough becomes hard to spread evenly, place the dish in the oven; after 5 to 10 minutes, the dough will soften and you'll be able to just shake the dish to get everything to even out. Bake for about 15 minutes, or until the dough turns light brown. Remove from the oven immediately once it reaches the right color to stop the cooking. Be careful not to overcook the dough. Let the cookie cool completely in the dish.

Once the cookie has cooled completely, invert the dish over parchment paper to remove the cookie. Use an offset spatula to spread a thin layer of white chocolate across the bottom in an even and flat layer. Let the cookie set in a cool, dry place until the chocolate firms up, about 30 minutes.

Once the chocolate is firm, place a piece of parchment paper over it and invert the cookie onto a cutting board. The parchment will keep the chocolate from sticking to the board. With a large chef's knife, cut the cookie into 1-by-2-inch bars. You can trim the edges of the whole cookie before cutting if you want to give the bars a neater appearance. Store the cookies in an airtight container in a cool, dry place for up to 1 week, with parchment paper between each layer to keep the cookies from sticking to each other.

Coconut-Walnut Cookies

MAKES ABOUT 40 COOKIES

These cookies, which have a slightly crunchy crust contrasted by a soft interior, take just minutes to prepare. Both the dough and the baked cookies can be frozen, tightly wrapped in plastic and stored in an airtight container, for up to a month.

9½ tablespoons (135 grams) unsalted butter, at room temperature

1 cup plus 1 tablespoon (130 grams) confectioners' sugar

1 large egg

3 cups (225 grams) unsweetened desiccated coconut

¾ cup (100 grams) all-purpose flour

1⅓ cups (150 grams) walnuts, chopped

1 teaspoon (5 grams) pure vanilla extract

Preheat the oven to 375°F (190°C) and line a baking sheet with parchment paper.

In the bowl of a stand mixer fitted with the paddle attachment, beat the butter and confectioners' sugar together on low speed until the mixture becomes pale and fluffy. Add the egg and mix until smooth. Add 2 cups (150 grams) of the coconut, the flour, walnuts, and vanilla, and mix until everything is fully combined.

Pour the remaining 1 cup (75 grams) coconut into a bowl. With your hands, roll the dough into quarter-size balls. Roll the balls in the coconut until they are completely coated, and place them on the baking sheet. Bake for 8 to 10 minutes, or until the edges and tops start to turn light brown. Remove the cookies from the oven, let them cool completely on the baking sheet, then store them in an airtight container in a cool, dry place for up to 2 days.

Pistachio-Almond Squares

MAKES ABOUT 96 ONE-INCH SQUARE COOKIES

These petits fours date back to my days at Restaurant Daniel, and they have been a big hit in my repertoire ever since. You can purchase pistachio paste in gourmet stores and online (see Resources, page 266), or make your own (see page 23 for the recipe). This sweet dough is an excellent base for all kinds of bar cookies, and is used again in this book for the Pecan Squares on page 103 and Florentine Bars on page 155.

SWEET DOUGH

8 ounces (225 grams) unsalted butter, at room temperature

½ cup plus 1 tablespoon (110 grams) granulated sugar

1 large egg

2 large egg yolks

2⅔ cups (340 grams) all-purpose flour

PISTACHIO-ALMOND CREAM

8 ounces plus 1½ tablespoons (250 grams) unsalted butter, at room temperature

1¼ cups (250 grams) granulated sugar

2½ cups (250 grams) almond flour

(continued)

MAKE THE SWEET DOUGH: In the bowl of a stand mixer fitted with the paddle attachment, beat the butter and sugar together on low speed until the mixture becomes pale and fluffy. Add the egg and egg yolks one at a time, waiting until each is fully incorporated before adding the next one, and mix until fully combined. Add the flour and mix until incorporated. Remove the dough from the bowl, wrap in plastic wrap, and refrigerate until it is chilled all the way through, a few hours or overnight.

Spray the sides and bottom of a 9-by-13-inch glass baking dish with nonstick cooking spray, then line it with parchment paper, covering the bottom and sides. Spray the paper with cooking spray.

On a floured surface, roll out the dough into a rectangle approximately 14 by 16 inches and ¼ inch thick. Roll the dough over your rolling pin and use the pin to drape the dough into the pan. If the dough cracks, simply press it back into place as you would for a tart shell. Press the dough into the bottom of the dish, its corners, and then up the sides. Generously prick the bottom and sides with a fork, then refrigerate or freeze for at least 1 hour, until the dough is chilled all the way through.

Preheat the oven to 375°F (190°C).

Once chilled, bake the dough for about 15 minutes, or until the crust turns a very light brown. You are only looking to parbake it,

6 large eggs

3 tablespoons (25 grams) all-purpose flour

2/3 cup (160 grams) pistachio paste

1 teaspoon (5 grams) pure vanilla extract

since it will bake again with the filling. Check the dough halfway through baking, at about 7 minutes, to make sure that it is not forming bubbles and pulling away from the dish. If it is, prick it again with a fork or press it down with your fingers. When done, remove from the oven and let the shell cool completely in the dish. Prick any remaining bubbles. You can parbake the shell up to 1 day ahead. If you do this, let cool, then wrap the whole dish in plastic wrap and store at room temperature.

MAKE THE PISTACHIO-ALMOND CREAM: In the bowl of a stand mixer fitted with the paddle attachment, beat the butter and sugar together on medium speed until the mixture is well combined and smooth. Add the almond flour and mix until well combined. Add the eggs two at a time (in three increments total), waiting until each is fully incorporated before adding the next, and mix until fully combined. Add the all-purpose flour, pistachio paste, and vanilla, and mix until very smooth. Store, covered, at room temperature until ready to use. If you make it more than a few hours ahead, cover it and refrigerate for up to 1 week; let it come to room temperature before using.

ASSEMBLE THE COOKIES: Lower the oven temperature (or preheat the oven if you parbaked the shell in advance) to 350°F (175°C).

Pour the pistachio-almond cream on top of the parbaked shell and use a silicone spatula to spread it as evenly as possible. Bake for 15 to 25 minutes, checking after 15 minutes and then at 5-minute intervals, until the pistachio-almond cream starts to spring back when touched. Remove from the oven and let cool completely in the baking dish.

Once cool, transfer the whole cookie to a cutting board. The sides will likely be a bit uneven, so trim about ½ inch from each side. You should have a rectangle of about 8 by 12 inches. Cut the cookies into 1-inch squares. Store the squares in an airtight container in a cool, dry place for up to 1 week, with a sheet of parchment or waxed paper between each layer.

Pecan Squares

MAKES ABOUT 96 ONE-INCH SQUARE COOKIES

One American dessert I came to love quickly after moving to New York is pecan pie, even though it is much sweeter than most French desserts. These cookies are my version of it, with the added convenience that a bar is generally smaller and more portable than a slice of pie. You can cut these into bars or squares of any size. If you plan on serving them as part of an assortment and to many people, cut them into 1-inch squares; if you want to give them as afternoon treats or part of a lunch box, for example, go for larger squares or bars.

CRUST

Sweet Dough (page 101)

FILLING

3 tablespoons (45 grams) unsalted butter

2 tablespoons (40 grams) honey

1½ cups (360 grams) heavy cream

1 teaspoon (5 grams) pure vanilla extract

1½ cups (360 grams) water

2 tablespoons (30 grams) freshly squeezed lemon juice

5 cups (1 kilogram) granulated sugar

¼ cup plus 1 tablespoon (75 grams) light corn syrup

8¼ cups (900 grams) pecans, toasted (see page 21)

MAKE THE CRUST: Fit the Sweet Dough into the bottom (but not up the sides) of a 9-by-13-inch glass baking dish and parbake as described on page 101. Let the crust cool completely in the dish.

If you prepared the crust ahead of time, preheat the oven to 375°F (190°C).

MAKE THE FILLING: In a medium saucepan over medium-high heat, bring the butter, honey, cream, and vanilla to a boil.

At the same time, in a large saucepan, combine the water, lemon juice, sugar, and corn syrup and cook over medium-high heat until the mixture turns into a light brown caramel, about 5 minutes.

Very gently, being careful not to let the caramel splatter and burn you, pour the hot cream mixture little by little (three additions are good) into the caramel. Bring the mixture to a boil, then remove from the heat and fold in the pecans.

Let the mixture cool slightly, then pour it over the parbaked crust. Bake for 10 to 12 minutes, or until the mixture sets. Let cool, then carefully invert from the baking dish onto a piece of waxed paper and cut into squares or bars. Store the squares in an airtight container in a cool, dry place for up to 1 week, with parchment or waxed paper between each layer.

Walnut Cookie Bars

MAKES ABOUT 50 TO 60 1¼-INCH BAR COOKIES

Like the Pistachio-Almond Squares (page 101) and Pecan Squares (page 103), these walnut cookies consist of filling poured over sweet dough—in this case, a caramel-based walnut filling topped with almond cream. The cookies' components can be prepared ahead (the walnut filling is easy to make the night before and can stay out at room temperature, so you don't even need refrigerator space). The cookies bake as one in the pan and then are easily sliced into individual portions, which makes them ideal when you need dessert for a crowd.

WALNUT FILLING

⅓ cup plus 2 tablespoons
(112 grams) water

1¼ cups (250 grams)
sugar

2⅓ cups (250 grams)
walnuts, chopped

1 cup (250 grams) heavy
cream

CRUST

Sweet Dough (page 101)

ALMOND CREAM

9 tablespoons (125 grams)
unsalted butter, at room
temperature

½ cup plus 1 tablespoon
(125 grams) granulated
sugar

1¼ cups (125 grams)
almond flour

(continued)

MAKE THE WALNUT FILLING: Pour the water into a medium saucepan, then carefully pour the sugar into the center of the pot. Turn the heat to medium-high, then bring the sugar to a boil, without stirring. Positioning the sugar in the center of the pot will help prevent it from crystalizing on the sides of the pot, which might in turn crystalize your caramel. Carefully watch the sugar; it will begin to caramelize around the pot's edges first. Once the caramelization begins, carefully swirl the pot to ensure that it proceeds evenly and that all the sugar caramelizes at the same time.

As soon as the caramel turns light brown, immediately turn off the heat and add the walnuts and the cream to the pot. Stand back because the mixture will splatter. With a wooden spoon, stir the mixture until it is well combined and the caramel is fully melted. If there are still chunks of caramel, heat the pot slowly over low heat and stir continuously until it is fully melted. Transfer to a glass or ceramic bowl and let it cool fully at room temperature, which may take a few hours. Store, covered, at room temperature until ready to use. If you make the caramel more than a few hours ahead, cover it and refrigerate for up to 1 week; let it come to room temperature the night before you plan to use it so that it can soften.

MAKE THE CRUST: Spray the sides and bottom of a 9-by-13-inch glass baking dish with nonstick cooking spray, then line it with parchment paper, covering the bottom and sides. Spray the paper with cooking spray.

3 large eggs

1 teaspoon (5 grams) pure vanilla extract

TOPPING

¼ cup (60 grams) apricot preserves, melted

55 to 65 whole walnut halves

Prepare the Sweet Dough, press it into the bottom and slighlty up the sides of the baking dish, and parbake as indicated on page 101.

MAKE THE ALMOND CREAM: In the bowl of a stand mixer fitted with the paddle attachment, beat the butter and sugar together on medium speed until the mixture is well combined and smooth. Add the almond flour and mix until well combined. Add the eggs one at a time, waiting until each is fully incorporated before adding the next, and mix until fully combined. Add the vanilla and mix until the mixture is very smooth. Store, covered, at room temperature until ready to use. If you make the almond cream more than a few hours ahead, cover it and refrigerate for up to 1 week; let it come to room temperature before using.

ASSEMBLE THE COOKIES: Preheat the oven to 350°F (175°C).

Pour the cooled walnut filling on top of the sweet dough and use a silicone spatula to spread it as evenly as possible. Do the same with the soft almond cream on top of the walnut filling, spreading it in an even layer. Bake for about 30 minutes, until the filling and the crust have both turned light golden brown. Remove from the oven and let cool completely in the baking dish.

Once cool, transfer the whole cookie to a cutting board. The sides will likely be a bit uneven, so trim about ½ inch from each side of the cookie. You should have a rectangle of about 8 by 12 inches. Brush the melted apricot preserves over the whole cookie to give it a glossy finish. With a large knife, cut the cookie into 1¼-inch squares and place a walnut half on top of each square. Store the squares in an airtight container in a cool, dry place for up to 1 week, placing a sheet of parchment or waxed paper between each layer.

Hazelnut-Pistachio Slices

MAKES 80 TO 100 COOKIES

I love cookies that have nuts in them, but not always with the nuts in big chunks (that's what biscotti are for). These cookies are very thin, so each contains only little bits of pistachios and hazelnuts. They go well with a fruit compote, such as plum or rhubarb.

2 cups minus
2 tablespoons (250 grams)
all-purpose flour

½ teaspoon (3 grams)
baking soda

Pinch of salt

4½ tablespoons
(65 grams) unsalted
butter, at room
temperature

¾ cup minus 1 tablespoon
(150 grams) light brown
sugar

3 tablespoons (45 grams)
water

⅔ cup (90 grams)
hazelnuts, finely chopped

¼ cup (30 grams)
pistachios, finely chopped

Grated zest of ½ lemon

Line a baking sheet with parchment paper.

Into a large bowl, sift together the flour, baking soda, and salt.

In a medium saucepan, heat the butter, brown sugar, and water over low heat. Cook, whisking, until everything is melted and combined and the mixture is slightly hot. Remove from the heat and pour the mixture over the dry ingredients, then stir in the hazelnuts, pistachios, and lemon zest. Mix until everything is fully incorporated. Let cool to room temperature, then remove the dough from the bowl and place on the baking sheet. Roll the dough out until it forms a square 1 inch thick (it should be about 5½ by 5½ inches). Cover it with plastic wrap and refrigerate until the dough is fully chilled, preferably overnight.

Preheat the oven to 350°F (175°C).

Transfer the chilled dough to a cutting board and, with a sharp knife, slice it into 1-inch-wide strips. Place the strips in the freezer for about 15 minutes, until they firm up again

Working with one strip at a time, cut the dough into ⅛-inch-thick slices. You should have 1-by-1-by-⅛-inch squares. Arrange the squares on the baking sheet (replace the parchment paper if needed) and bake for about 10 minutes, or until the cookies just begin to turn a light brown color on the bottom. Remove the cookies from the oven and let them cool completely on the baking sheet or a cooling rack, then store them in an airtight container in a cool, dry place for up to 2 weeks.

Loaded Nut Slices

MAKES ABOUT 45 COOKIES

These cookies are almost like biscotti, but unlike them, they are only baked once. I like them because they are very crunchy and crumbly and they go well with ice cream. They also combine almonds, hazelnuts, and pistachios, which is rare. They are sliced from a log that you can keep frozen, tightly wrapped in plastic and stored in an airtight container, for up to a month. You can also press the dough into a baking sheet, shaping into a large rectangle about 1½ inches thick, then cut them to give them a squarer shape closer to the photo on page 106. Because they are filled with an assortment of nuts, when they are cut, no two slices will look perfectly alike. You could also shape the dough into balls or scoop it onto the baking sheet, rather than slicing it, for rounder cookies. Serve them as part of a cookie platter, as pictured, or on their own with a cup of Earl Grey tea.

10½ tablespoons (150 grams) unsalted butter, at room temperature

1¾ cups (200 grams) confectioners' sugar

2 cups minus 2 tablespoons (250 grams) all-purpose flour

1½ cups (150 grams) almond flour

1 teaspoon (5 grams) baking powder

1 large egg white

2 teaspoons (10 grams) heavy cream

2 teaspoons (10 grams) dark rum, such as Myers's

(continued)

In the bowl of a stand mixer fitted with the paddle attachment, beat the butter and confectioners' sugar together on low speed until the mixture becomes pale and fluffy. Add the all-purpose flour, almond flour, and baking powder and mix until smooth. Slowly drizzle in the egg white, cream, rum, and vanilla. Once combined, add the pistachios, almonds, hazelnuts, and raisins and mix until everything is fully combined. The dough will become very stiff, so you might need to turn off your mixer and finish folding in the nuts with a silicone spatula.

Remove the dough from the bowl and divide it into two pieces. Place each piece of dough on plastic wrap and roll it into logs that are about 1½ inches in diameter. Refrigerate for about 2 hours, or until the logs are chilled all the way through.

> LOADED NUT SLICES, THIS PAGE, PAIN TURC, PAGE 111, AND CINNAMON COOKIES, PAGE 112

2 teaspoons (10 grams) pure vanilla extract

½ cup (60 grams) pistachios, toasted (see page 21)

⅓ cup (45 grams) almonds, toasted (see page 21)

⅓ cup (45 grams) hazelnuts, toasted (see page 21)

⅓ cup (50 grams) golden raisins

Preheat the oven to 350°F (175°C) and line a baking sheet with parchment paper.

With a sharp knife, slice the logs into ¼-inch-thick slices and arrange them on the baking sheet. Bake for 10 to 12 minutes, or until they begin to turn a light golden brown color. Remove the cookies from the oven and let them cool completely on the baking sheet or a cooling rack, then store them in an airtight container in a cool, dry place for up to 2 weeks.

Pain Turc

MAKES ABOUT 80 COOKIES

The name pain turc, *or "Turkish bread," refers to the fact that these cookies contain almonds. And* pain *(bread), it is what we commonly use in France when referring to sliced cookies, since they are cut like slices of bread before being baked. You can freeze the dough, tightly wrapped in plastic and stored in an airtight container, for up to a month. The key to this simple dough is not to incorporate too much air into the batter, or the cookies will spread and break because of their high butter content. You might even prefer to mix them by hand rather than in the stand mixer. The cookies should have a light, airy, and crumbly consistency.*

14 tablespoons (200 grams) unsalted butter, at room temperature

2 cups plus 1 tablespoon (250 grams) confectioners' sugar

1 teaspoon (4 grams) salt

1 large egg

1½ cups plus 1 tablespoon (200 grams) all-purpose flour

2⅔ cups (230 grams) sliced almonds, toasted (see page 21)

Line a baking sheet with parchment paper.

In the bowl of a stand mixer fitted with the paddle attachment, beat the butter, confectioners' sugar, and salt together on low speed just until combined. Mix in the egg until combined, then add the flour and almonds and mix until combined.

Place the dough on the baking sheet. Roll the dough out until it forms a square 1 inch thick (it should be about 6½ by 6½ inches). Cover it with plastic wrap and refrigerate until fully chilled, preferably overnight.

Preheat the oven to 350°F (175°C).

Transfer the chilled dough to a cutting board and, with a sharp knife, slice it into 1-inch-wide strips. Place the strips in the freezer for about 15 minutes, until they firm up again.

Working with one strip at a time, cut the dough into ¼-inch-thick slices. You should have 1-by-1-by-¼-inch squares. Arrange the squares on the baking sheet (replace the parchment paper if needed) and bake for about 10 minutes, or until the cookies just begin to turn a light brown color on the bottom. Remove the cookies from the oven and let them cool completely on the baking sheet or a cooling rack, then store them in an airtight container in a cool, dry place for up to 2 weeks.

Cinnamon Cookies

MAKES ABOUT 60 COOKIES

A cinnamon-sugar mixture goes so well on things like waffles, apple pies, or even just toast that I figured, why not put it on a cookie! It's a rare flavor to find in France, so this is really more my American adaptation of a speculoos cookie, a Dutch and Belgian specialty that has made its way through France, first only in the north close to the Belgium border but now is found everywhere. It is a butter cookie with a hint of lemon inside, in addition to the spice, with a nice flaky texture. You slice the chilled or frozen dough, sprinkle the cinnamon topping over the slices, and bake. I love serving them in the fall with a hot cup of apple cider.

DOUGH

12½ tablespoons (175 grams) unsalted butter, at room temperature

¼ cup plus 2 tablespoons (80 grams) granulated sugar

⅓ cup (70 grams) light brown sugar

Grated zest of 1 lemon

2⅓ cups (320 grams) all-purpose flour

1 teaspoon (5 grams) baking powder

1 tablespoon (5 grams) ground cinnamon

1 tablespoon plus 1 teaspoon (20 grams) vegetable oil

1 teaspoon (5 grams) water

(continued)

MAKE THE DOUGH: Preheat the oven to 350°F (175°C) and line a baking sheet with parchment paper.

In the bowl of a stand mixer fitted with the paddle attachment, beat the butter, granulated sugar, brown sugar, and lemon zest together on low speed until the mixture becomes pale and fluffy. Add the flour, baking powder, and cinnamon and mix until combined, then add the oil and water and mix until fully combined.

Place the dough on plastic wrap and roll it into logs that are 2 inches in diameter. Smaller logs are easier to work with than one long one. Twist the ends of the plastic wrap as you would to wrap a candy to help you achieve an evenly round log. Freeze for about 2 hours, or until the logs are chilled all the way through. You can freeze the logs, well wrapped in plastic and stored in an airtight container, for up to 1 month.

¼ cup (50 grams)
granulated sugar

1 tablespoon plus
1 teaspoon (10 grams)
ground cinnamon

MAKE THE TOPPING: In a small bowl, whisk together the granulated sugar and cinnamon until well combined.

With a sharp knife, slice the logs into ¼-inch-thick slices and arrange them on the baking sheet. Sprinkle with the cinnamon-sugar mixture, then bake for about 10 minutes, or until the cookies begin to pick up a little color along the bottom edges. Remove the cookies from the oven and let them cool completely on the baking sheet or a cooling rack, then store them in an airtight container in a cool, dry place for up to 1 week.

Brown Sugar Spiced Cookies

MAKES ABOUT 40 COOKIES

Like the Cinnamon Cookies on page 112, these are topped with a spiced sugar mixture, but they are rolled and cut into shapes rather than sliced. You can use any shape cookie cutter you'd like, but the size may change the final number of cookies. If you prefer the convenience of "slice and bake" cookies, you can also roll the dough into logs that are 2 to 3 inches in diameter, chill them, then slice and bake them.

DOUGH

8 ounces plus
5 tablespoons (300 grams)
unsalted butter, at room
temperature

1 cup plus 1 tablespoon
(220 grams) light brown
sugar

3½ cups all-purpose flour

1 teaspoon (2 grams)
five-spice powder

1 teaspoon (4 grams) salt

½ teaspoon (2.5 grams)
pure vanilla extract

TOPPING

¼ cup (55 grams) light
brown sugar

1 teaspoon (2 grams)
five-spice powder

MAKE THE DOUGH: In the bowl of a stand mixer fitted with the paddle attachment, beat the butter and brown sugar together on low speed until the mixture becomes pale and fluffy. Add the flour, five-spice powder, salt, and vanilla and mix very gently until everything is incorporated.

Transfer the dough to a sheet of parchment paper and cover with another sheet. Roll out the dough between the sheets of parchment until it is about ¼ inch thick. Cover the dough with plastic wrap and refrigerate until fully chilled, about 2 hours.

Preheat the oven to 375°F (190°C).

MAKE THE TOPPING: In a small bowl, whisk together the brown sugar and five-spice powder until well combined.

With a 2-inch round cookie cutter, cut out circles of dough and place them on the lined baking sheet, rerolling the scraps as necessary. Sprinkle with the topping, then bake for 8 to 12 minutes, or until the cookies turn a light brown color. Remove the cookies from the oven and let them cool completely on the baking sheet or a cooling rack, then store them in an airtight container in a cool, dry place for up to 1 week.

Cardamom Viennois

MAKES ABOUT 80 COOKIES

Traditionally, Viennois are S-shaped vanilla cookies—perfect companions to a cup of coffee. But I like to flavor them with cardamom instead, a complexly flavored spice often found in Swedish baked goods, in Indian foods, and in chai, and serve them with tea. They are easier to make when piped in a straight line or as rosettes, as in the recipe instructions here, but if you want to make them in their classic shape, pipe the dough into an S shape.

14 ounces plus ½ tablespoon (400 grams) unsalted butter, at room temperature

1¼ cups (150 grams) confectioners' sugar

2 large egg whites

3½ cups (450 grams) all-purpose flour

2 teaspoons (4 grams) ground cardamom

1 teaspoon (4 grams) salt

¼ cup (20 grams) sliced almonds

Preheat the oven to 350°F (175°C) and line a baking sheet with parchment paper.

In the bowl of a stand mixer fitted with the paddle attachment, beat the butter and confectioners' sugar together on low speed until just combined. Mix in the egg whites until just combined, then add the flour, cardamom, and salt and mix until just combined.

With a spatula, transfer the mixture to a pastry bag fitted with a ½-inch star pastry tip. Pipe the dough onto the lined baking sheet in straight lines 2 inches long or in rosettes, then press 2 sliced almonds onto the top of each cookie. Bake for about 10 minutes, or until the cookies turn a light golden brown color. Remove the cookies from the oven and let them cool completely on the baking sheet or a cooling rack, then store them in an airtight container in a cool, dry place for up to 2 weeks.

Allumettes aux Épices

MAKES ABOUT 30 COOKIES

These cookies combine a flaky layer of puff pastry with spiced icing, which means that their edges and bottom are crispy while the center remains slightly soft and moist. Their name, allumettes, refers to a matchstick shape, but you can cut them into any shape you'd like, such as stars for the holidays or hearts for Valentine's Day. Five-spice is a Chinese spice blend that typically includes cinnamon, cloves, anise, star anise, and ginger. In such a simple recipe, I like the very complex flavor it gives the icing. You can also vary the spices you use, adding, for example, cinnamon or cardamom. Use store-bought puff pastry, or the Quick Puff Pastry on page 58. These are best eaten the day they are made. Baking them on an inverted baking sheet allows you to both apply the icing and cut the dough into individual pieces more easily.

---

1 pound (450 grams) puff pastry, thawed

1 large egg white

¾ cup plus 1 tablespoon (100 grams) confectioners' sugar

2 tablespoons (15 grams) five-spice powder

1 tablespoon (6 grams) ground cloves

Line an inverted baking sheet with parchment paper.

Roll out the puff pastry until it is ⅛ inch thick, keeping it in a rectangle shape the size of the baking sheet, then place on the inverted baking sheet and prick all over with a fork. Freeze it for about 1 hour, or until it is firm.

Preheat the oven to 400°F (205°C).

In the bowl of a stand mixer fitted with the paddle attachment, beat the egg white, confectioners' sugar, five-spice powder, and cloves on high speed until well combined and enough air has been incorporated to make for a thick icing that is still spreadable but not runny. You will need to lift the bowl at the beginning of the process to ensure that the paddle can reach the mixture.

Remove the puff pastry from the freezer and use an offset spatula to spread a very thin layer of icing over the whole pastry. Return to the freezer for about 5 minutes, until the icing firms up. It will be easier to cut into matchsticks when chilled.

Move the puff pastry to a cutting board and cut it into 1-by-5-inch strips: You should be able to cut the pastry across the middle horizontally and then cut each half vertically into 15 one-inch pieces. Transfer the strips back to the baking sheet (change the parchment paper if necessary).

Bake for 15 to 20 minutes, or until the icing is light brown and the puff pastry is light brown and crispy on the edges. Remove from the oven and let cool completely on the baking sheet.

Almond Gommés

MAKES ABOUT 50 COOKIES

Gommés earned their names because they were traditionally made with gum arabic, which gave them their chewiness. I remember my father making them that way when I was young and working at his pastry shop in France. Nowadays, I use almond flour instead, but I still like using the name, especially since they still have a chewy texture. I make a lot of these around Passover since they don't contain any flour and, because they keep for a long time, help defray last-minute holiday stress. They are also perfect if you cannot consume gluten.

2½ cups (250 grams) almond flour

1¼ cups (250 grams) granulated sugar

3 large egg whites

½ cup (85 grams) finely chopped candied orange peel (see page 120)

50 to 60 whole blanched almonds

Preheat the oven to 350°F (180°C) and line a baking sheet with parchment paper.

In a food processor, grind together the almond flour, sugar, egg whites, and candied orange peel until the mixture is very smooth.

With a spatula, transfer the dough to a pastry bag fitted with a ½-inch star pastry tip. Pipe into 1-inch shells: Start by piping a star, then move the pastry bag to lengthen the shape into an elongated shell, decreasing the pressure on the dough to form a narrow point as you lift the pastry bag. Place a whole blanched almond on top of each cookie. Bake for 12 to 15 minutes, or until the cookies turn a light golden brown color. Remove the cookies from the oven, let them cool completely on the baking sheet or a cooling rack, then store them in an airtight container in a cool, dry place for up to 2 weeks, or freeze them, wrapped in plastic and in an airtight container, for up to 1 month (remove them from the freezer a few hours before serving to bring to room temperature).

< ALMOND GOMMÉS, THIS PAGE, CHERRY GOMMÉS, PAGE 121, AND ORANGE GOMMÉS, PAGE 122

Candied Orange, Lemon, or Grapefruit Peel

1 orange, lemon, or grapefruit, scrubbed thoroughly

1¼ cups (250 grams) granulated sugar

1 tablespoon (17 grams) light corn syrup

½ cup (120 grams) water

Cut the orange, lemon, or grapefruit into quarters. Remove the pulp and as much of the white pith as possible. Place the peels in a medium saucepan, fill it with water, and bring to a boil. Drain the water, then fill the pot with fresh water and bring to a boil again. Drain and repeat this process a third time. Drain the water completely.

Combine the peels, sugar, and corn syrup with the ½ cup (120 grams) water in the saucepan, and place over low heat. Simmer for about 1 hour, or until the peels become slightly translucent. Remove from the heat, and let the peels cool in the syrup. You can store the peels in the syrup, covered and refrigerated, for up to 2 weeks.

Cherry Gommés

Don't be tempted to make this recipe with the fancy cocktail maraschino cherries. They contain too much liquid, which will leak onto the cookies and stain them. Look for the classic confectionery cherries that are dyed bright red or green and are drier; you will need about 50. The color scheme makes these perfect holiday cookies.

Gommé dough (page 119)

About 50 candied cherries

Prepare the dough as instructed on page 119 (omit the whole blanched almonds). With a spatula, transfer the dough to a pastry bag fitted with a ½-inch star pastry tip. Pipe into 1-inch rosettes, then place a red or green cherry at the center of each cookie. Bake for 12 to 15 minutes, or until the cookies turn a light golden brown color. Remove the cookies from the oven, let them cool completely on the baking sheet or a cooling rack, then store them in an airtight container in a cool, dry place for up to 2 weeks, or freeze them, wrapped in plastic and in an airtight container, for up to 1 month.

Orange Gommés

The candied orange peel that adorns these cookies reinforces the orange flavor of the dough. Use candied lemon or grapefruit peels, or even candied ginger, as variations.

Gommé dough (page 119)

35 two-inch strips candied orange peel (page 120)

Prepare the dough as instructed on page 119 (omit the whole blanched almonds). With a spatula, transfer the dough to a pastry bag fitted with a ½-inch star pastry tip. Pipe into 1-inch shells, and then pipe a second shell slightly overlapping the first one, for a total length of 2 inches. Place a piece of candied orange peel over the length of the cookie, and bake for 12 to 15 minutes, or until the cookies turn a light golden brown color. Remove the cookies from the oven, let them cool completely on the baking sheet or a cooling rack, then store them in an airtight container in a cool, dry place for up to 2 weeks, or freeze them, wrapped in plastic and in an airtight container, for up to 1 month.

Christmas Balls

MAKES 35 TO 40 COOKIES

I like offering these cookies as alternatives to fruitcakes during the holidays. They contain candied and dried fruits, but their small, individual serving size means that guests won't get full on just one type of dessert. They look like little snowballs and are beautiful as part of an assortment of cookies on a table or buffet (with other gommés, for example).

2½ cups (250 grams) almond flour

1¼ cups (250 grams) granulated sugar

4 large egg whites

¼ cup plus 2 tablespoons (70 grams) finely chopped candied orange peel (page 120)

1 tablespoon (15 grams) finely chopped candied ginger

¼ cup plus 1 tablespoon (50 grams) dried cranberries

2 cups (240 grams) confectioners' sugar

In a food processor, grind together the almond flour, granulated sugar, egg whites, candied orange peel, and ginger until the mixture is very smooth. Add the cranberries and process just until fully combined. Wrap the dough in plastic wrap and refrigerate until it is chilled through, about 1 hour.

Preheat the oven to 350°F (180°C) and line a baking sheet with parchment paper.

Pour the confectioners' sugar into a bowl. With your hands, roll the dough into quarter-size balls. Roll the balls in the confectioners' sugar until they are completely coated, and place them on the baking sheet. Bake for 12 to 15 minutes, or until the cookies turn a light golden brown color. Remove the cookies from the oven, let them cool completely on the baking sheet, then store them in an airtight container in a cool, dry place for up to 2 weeks, or freeze them, wrapped in plastic and in an airtight container, for up to 1 month.

Chocolate Chip–Almond Balls

MAKES 35 TO 40 COOKIES

Sometimes you want just a bit of chocolate, not too much of it; these cookies, which combine chocolate chips with candied orange and grapefruit peels, offer just that. They are very easy to make and can be frozen, and they have a sophisticated look and flavor, so they are ideal to make ahead and keep on hand for holiday entertaining or for unexpected visitors.

2½ cups (250 grams) almond flour

1¼ cups (250 grams) granulated sugar

4 large egg whites

¼ cup plus 1 tablespoon (50 grams) finely chopped candied orange peel (page 120)

¼ cup plus 1 tablespoon (50 grams) finely chopped candied grapefruit peel (page 120)

⅓ cup (65 grams) mini chocolate chips

2½ cups (215 grams) sliced almonds

In a food processor, grind together the almond flour, sugar, egg whites, candied orange peel, and candied grapefruit peel until the mixture is very smooth. Add the chocolate chips and process just until fully combined. Wrap the dough in plastic wrap and refrigerate until it is chilled through, about 1 hour.

Preheat the oven to 350°F (180°C) and line a baking sheet with parchment paper.

Pour the sliced almonds into a bowl. With your hands, roll the dough into quarter-size balls. Roll the balls in the almonds until they are completely coated, and place them on the baking sheet. Bake for 12 to 15 minutes, or until the cookies turn a light golden brown color. Remove the cookies from the oven, let them cool completely on the baking sheet, then store them in an airtight container in a cool, dry place for up to 2 weeks, or freeze them, wrapped in plastic and in an airtight container, for up to 1 month.

Financiers & Tea Cakes

Financiers are among the most classic of French cookies. They have a soft, delicate consistency that is almost cake-like, and are usually made with browned butter and nuts, which gives them their name, since those were at one time luxury ingredients. You'll often find them on a plate of *mignardises*, the little treats brought with coffee or the bill in high-end restaurants in both France and the United States, but in truth they are among the easiest cookies to make. Everything goes into one bowl, chills overnight so that the flour can relax, and the next day you just have to bake them. Financier molds, often made out of silicone, are available in kitchenware stores and online (see Resources, page 266). The classic shape is rectangular, but you'll find more and more round financiers because they stay moister and are thicker in that shape. Because the following pages include several financier recipes, buying a financier mold would be a worthy investment. You can also use a mini muffin pan lined with paper baking cups; those financiers will be a bit larger, so you might get fewer cookies out of the recipes, but they will be just as delicious.

Almond-Vanilla Financiers

MAKES 40 TO 50 FINANCIERS

These financiers have a very delicate flavor, coming from the almond flour and vanilla extract in the batter. As a result, they are the perfect accompaniment to a cup of equally delicate tea, such as jasmine or Darjeeling. Present them in a bag tied with a beautiful ribbon when visiting friends—a hostess gift that will guarantee you are invited back. For an extra flourish, top each financier with an almond or other nut or a small piece of dried or candied fruit before baking. This batter will make enough to fill at least two 20-count financier molds, but no need to buy two: The batter can sit while one batch bakes without any issues.

14 tablespoons (200 grams) unsalted butter

1 cup plus 3 tablespoons (240 grams) granulated sugar

1 cup plus 2 teaspoons (100 grams) almond flour

¾ cup (80 grams) all-purpose flour

1½ teaspoons (6 grams) baking powder

7 large egg whites

1 tablespoon (15 grams) pure vanilla extract

Confectioners' sugar, for dusting

Place the butter in a small saucepan over medium-high heat. Let it bubble and cook until it turns light golden brown. Whisk a couple times during the process to ensure that all the butter melts and browns evenly. Once it reaches the desired light brown color, immediately remove from the heat.

Into a medium bowl, sift together the granulated sugar, almond flour, all-purpose flour, and baking powder, then whisk until they are evenly combined. Whisk in the egg whites and vanilla until just combined. Pour in the hot butter and whisk until everything is fully combined. If you wish, transfer the batter to a large measuring cup (which makes it easier to pour into the mold), or leave in the bowl; cover, and refrigerate for at least 2 hours, or preferably overnight, to allow the flour to relax.

Preheat the oven to 375°F (190°C). Spray a silicone financier mold with nonstick cooking spray or line a mini muffin pan with paper baking cups. If using a silicone mold, place it on a baking sheet.

Stir the batter, then pour just enough of it to fill the individual molds or muffin cups three-quarters full. If you prefer to pipe the batter, which is a more precise way to fill the small molds, transfer it to a pastry bag fitted with a ¼-inch round pastry tip. You can also just cut a ¼-inch opening into the tip of the pastry bag, and then pipe the batter into the molds. Bake for about 20 minutes, or until the financiers are light golden brown, spring back when you lightly press on them, and a toothpick inserted in the center comes out clean. Remove from the oven, let them cool completely in the mold, then store them in an airtight container in a cool, dry place for up to 2 days. Dust them with confectioners' sugar before serving.

Papa's Financiers

MAKES 40 TO 50 FINANCIERS

My father was as fond of financiers as I am, and he created this unique take on them. The steps are very minimal, but there are waiting periods between them, so this is not a cookie you can decide to make on a whim and be ready to serve 30 minutes later. I promise you, though, that you will not regret any of the wait when you bite into your first one. You need to prepare the nut-flour mixture the day before baking them, to allow the oil from the almonds to separate. Stir the mixture well before using to incorporate the oil back into the mixture. If you don't wait a day, the oil will come out in the finished financiers, resulting in an unpleasant texture. Like the other financier recipes in this chapter, you will have enough batter to fill multiple molds, but you can let the batter sit while one batch is in the oven.

---

2 cups plus 1 tablespoon (200 grams) almond flour

¾ cup plus 3 tablespoons (100 grams) whole unskinned almonds

7 tablespoons (90 grams) granulated sugar

¼ cup (30 grams) all-purpose flour

14 tablespoons (200 grams) unsalted butter

7 large egg whites

In a food processor, grind together the almond flour, almonds, sugar, and all-purpose flour until the mixture is smooth. Cover the bowl with plastic wrap, and let the mixture rest overnight.

Place the butter in a small saucepan over medium-high heat. Let it bubble and cook until it turns light golden brown. Whisk a couple of times during the process to ensure that all the butter melts and browns evenly. Once it reaches the desired light brown color, immediately remove from the heat.

Pour the hot butter and egg whites into the food processor on top of the nut-flour mixture, and process until everything is smooth. Transfer to a bowl or large measuring cup (which makes it easier to pour in the mold), cover, and refrigerate for 2 hours, to prevent the financiers from puffing up when you bake them.

Preheat the oven to 375°F (190°C). Spray a silicone financier mold with nonstick cooking spray or line a mini muffin pan with paper baking cups. If using a silicone mold, place it on a baking sheet.

Stir the batter, then pour just enough of it to fill the individual molds or muffin cups three-quarters full. If you prefer to pipe the batter, which is a more precise way to fill the small molds, transfer the batter to a pastry bag fitted with a ¼-inch round pastry tip. You can also just cut a ¼-inch opening into the tip of the pastry bag. Bake for 12 to 14 minutes, or until the financiers are light golden brown, spring back when you lightly press on them, and a toothpick inserted in the center comes out clean. Remove from the oven, let them cool completely in the mold, then store them in an airtight container in a cool, dry place for up to 2 days.

Apricot Financiers

A piece of fruit in the middle adds texture, moistness, and flavor to a simple financier. Instead of apricots, you could make them with canned peaches, pears, or pineapples if you prefer, or even with fruits that you have poached in syrup yourself until they are soft, such as plums or nectarines. Just make sure to drain the fruits so that they don't add too much liquid to the batter.

7 tablespoons (100 grams) unsalted butter

14 ounces (400 grams) almond paste

4 large eggs

Pinch of salt

15 canned apricot halves in syrup, drained (about one-and-a-half 15-ounce cans)

Place the butter in a small saucepan over medium-high heat. Let it bubble and cook until it turns light golden brown. Whisk a couple of times during the process to ensure that all the butter melts and browns evenly. Once it reaches the desired light brown color, immediately remove from the heat.

In a food processor, grind together the almond paste, eggs, salt, and 10 of the apricot halves until the mixture is smooth. Slowly drizzle in the hot butter, and mix until fully combined. Transfer to a bowl or large measuring cup (which makes it easier to pour in the mold), cover, and refrigerate for at least 3 hours, or preferably overnight.

Preheat the oven to 375°F (190°C). Spray a silicone financier mold with nonstick cooking spray or line a mini muffin pan with paper baking cups. If using a silicone mold, place it on a baking sheet.

Slice the remaining 5 apricot halves lengthwise into ¼-inch strips. Stir the batter, then pour just enough of it to fill the individual molds or muffin cups three-quarters full. If you prefer to pipe the batter, which is a more precise way to fill the small molds, transfer it to a pastry bag fitted with a ¼-inch round pastry tip. Arrange an apricot slice on top of each financier. Bake for 30 to 40 minutes, or until the financiers are light golden brown and a toothpick inserted in the center comes out clean. Remove from the oven, let them cool completely in the mold, then store them in an airtight container in a cool, dry place for up to 2 days.

Pistachio Financiers

MAKES 40 TO 50 FINANCIERS

Pistachio and chocolate is one of my favorite combinations, and it works like a charm in this financier. A portion of the batter is mixed with cocoa powder before baking, and ends up forming a chocolate center in the financier. Almond paste, which is used instead of almond flour in this recipe, can be hard to grind into a smooth texture, even in the food processor. If it is really stiff, you can grate it first before placing it in the food processor. It also helps to warm up and soften the paste by massaging it in your hands before grinding it. This batter is thick, so it'll be easier to pipe it rather than try to pour it into the molds.

7 tablespoons (100 grams) unsalted butter

14 ounces (400 grams) almond paste

5 tablespoons (80 grams) pistachio paste

4 large eggs

1½ tablespoons (9 grams) Dutch-process cocoa powder

Place the butter in a small saucepan over medium-high heat. Let it bubble and cook until it turns light golden brown. Whisk a couple of times during the process to ensure that all the butter melts and browns evenly. Once it reaches the desired light brown color, immediately remove from the heat.

In a food processor, grind together the almond paste and pistachio paste until the mixture is smooth, then add the eggs and process until combined. Slowly drizzle in the hot butter, and mix until fully combined. Spoon out about ¾ cup of batter (read carefully, *not* three-quarters of the batter!) into a small bowl and stir in the cocoa powder.

Transfer the rest of the plain pistachio batter to another bowl, cover both batters, and refrigerate for at least 3 hours, or preferably overnight.

Preheat the oven to 350°F (175°C). Spray a silicone financier mold with nonstick cooking spray or line a mini muffin pan with paper baking cups. If using a silicone mold, place it on a baking sheet.

Stir the plain batter, then, with a spatula, transfer it to a pastry bag fitted with a ¼-inch round pastry tip. You can also just cut a ¼-inch opening into the tip of the pastry bag. Pipe just enough of the batter to fill the individual molds or muffin cups three-quarters full.

Stir the chocolate batter and spoon in a small drop (about ¾ teaspoon) at the center of each financier (you can pipe it if you prefer, using a different pastry bag). It should sink into the plain batter as it bakes. Bake for about 30 minutes, or until the financiers are light golden brown, spring back when pressed, and a toothpick inserted in the center comes out clean. Remove from the oven, let them cool completely in the mold, then store them in an airtight container in a cool, dry place for up to 2 days.

Poppy Seed Financiers

MAKES 20 TO 25 FINANCIERS

Lemon and poppy seed is a combination I see mostly in muffins and loaf cakes in the United States, but I find that it works so well that I decided to turn it into financiers. The poppy seeds crunch slightly when you bite into the cookies, and the lemon zest shines through the almond flour. These are perfect with a cup of black or green tea.

4 tablespoons (57 grams) unsalted butter

⅔ cup (60 grams) almond flour

¼ cup (33 grams) all-purpose flour

¼ cup (50 grams) granulated sugar

¼ cup (30 grams) confectioners' sugar

Grated zest of 2 lemons

2 tablespoons (20 grams) poppy seeds

3 large egg whites

Place the butter in a small saucepan over medium-high heat. Let it bubble and cook until it turns light golden brown. Whisk a couple of times during the process to ensure that all the butter melts and browns evenly. Once it reaches the desired light brown color, immediately remove from the heat.

Into a medium bowl, sift together the almond flour, all-purpose flour, granulated sugar, and confectioners' sugar. Add the lemon zest and poppy seeds and whisk until evenly combined. Whisk in the egg whites until just combined. Pour in the hot butter and whisk until everything is fully combined. Transfer to a bowl or large measuring cup (which makes it easier to pour in the mold), cover, and refrigerate for at least 2 hours, or preferably overnight, to allow the flour to relax.

Preheat the oven to 375°F (190°C). Spray a silicone financier mold with nonstick cooking spray or line a mini muffin pan with paper baking cups. If using a silicone mold, place it on a baking sheet.

Stir the batter, then pour just enough of it to fill the individual molds or muffin cups three-quarters full, or transfer it to a pastry bag fitted with a ¼-inch round pastry tip. Bake for about 20 minutes, or until the financiers are light golden brown, spring back when you lightly press on them, and a toothpick inserted in the center comes out clean. Remove from the oven, let them cool completely in the mold, then store them in an airtight container in a cool, dry place for up to 2 days.

Coconut Financiers

MAKES 20 TO 25 FINANCIERS

This is a different type of financier, which doesn't include almond flour or even all-purpose flour. Instead, it is made with unsweetened coconut and comes closer to a macaroon. You will need to spoon the batter into the financier molds or mini muffin pans, since the coconut would get stuck in the tip of a piping bag. Be careful that no coconut flakes stick up from the mold or they will darken much faster than the batter will bake.

¼ cup plus 3 tablespoons (100 grams) whole milk

½ cup (100 grams) granulated sugar

2 cups (150 grams) unsweetened desiccated coconut

2 large eggs

Heat the milk in a medium saucepan over medium heat. Add the sugar and whisk until it has dissolved. Remove from the heat. Whisk in the coconut, then the eggs one at a time.

Preheat the oven to 350°F (175°C). Spray a silicone financier mold with nonstick cooking spray or line a mini muffin pan with paper baking cups. If using a silicone mold, place it on a baking sheet.

Spoon just enough of the batter into the individual molds or muffin cups to fill them three-quarters full. Push down any coconut flakes that stick up and flatten the top of the batter in each mold cavity. Bake for 12 to 15 minutes, or until the financiers are light golden brown. Remove from the oven, let them cool completely in the mold, then serve or store them in an airtight container in a cool, dry place for up to 2 days.

Assorted Tea Cakes

MAKES 48 TEA CAKES

These tea cakes are a canvas for almost any flavor of garnish you might want. Instead of the recommendations below, you could use dried cranberries, figs, or dates, or nuts such as almonds or pistachios (you will need about a cup), or serve them plain. The dough, made with two egg yolks in addition to the whole eggs, is richer than that of a financier. If you are using pineapple, dust with confectioners' sugar just before baking, or it will crack.

BATTER

11 ounces (325 grams) almond paste

3 large eggs

2 large egg yolks

⅓ cup (40 grams) all-purpose flour

7 tablespoons (100 grams) unsalted butter, melted

FOR PINEAPPLE TEA CAKES

One 8-ounce (225-gram) can pineapple slices or chunks, drained and cut into small pieces

FOR CHOCOLATE TEA CAKES

1 cup (210 grams) mini chocolate chips

FOR CANDIED ORANGE TEA CAKES

1 cup (160 grams) sliced candied orange (page 120)

Confectioners' sugar, for dusting

Preheat the oven to 375°F (190°C). Line a mini muffin pan with paper baking cups.

In the bowl of a stand mixer fitted with the paddle attachment, beat the almond paste on medium speed for a couple of minutes to slightly soften it. Add the eggs and the egg yolks one at a time, waiting until each is fully incorporated before adding the next, and mix until fully combined. Don't go too fast or the mixture might get lumpy. Reduce the mixer speed to low, mix in the flour, then slowly drizzle in the butter and mix until the batter is smooth.

With a spatula, transfer the batter to a pastry bag fitted with a ½-inch pastry tip. You can also just cut a ½-inch opening into the tip of the pastry bag. Pipe just enough of the batter to fill the muffin cups three-quarters full. Place a few pieces of pineapple, chocolate chips, or candied orange slices on top of the batter and dust with confectioners' sugar. Bake for about 20 minutes, or until the tea cakes are light golden brown and a toothpick inserted in the center comes out clean. Remove from the oven, let them cool completely in the pan, then store them in an airtight container in a cool, dry place for up to 2 days.

Tuiles & Florentines

Tuiles and florentines are both types of cookies that involve cooking sugar to a certain degree of chewiness. Tuiles are very thin and delicate and are often shaped around a rolling pin or bottle to give them a curly shape. They are meant to resemble old-fashioned tiles—which is what *tuiles* translates to in English. Florentines are thicker and contain nuts and often dried fruits in their caramelized base. Florentines can be time-consuming to make if you coat them in chocolate, as they are often sold, but the bar recipe I give you here offers the same great taste in a very easy method. As for tuiles, the key with them is to shape them very quickly while they are still hot. Until you get the hang of it, only bake two or three at a time to allow you enough time to shape them. As you become more experienced, you'll work up to baking ten to twelve at a time. But don't let their shape stress you out—they will be just as good flat if you decide not to bend them. You can also press tuiles into a small bowl or around a cone shape to form them into cups and ice cream cones for a special dessert.

Coconut Tuiles

MAKES ABOUT 28 TUILES

I love serving these coconut tuiles alongside chocolate ice cream or sorbet—a flavor pairing that always works. Not only are they an alternative to the more expected almond tuile or butter cookie, but they also hold up well to the weight of the ice cream when I use some of the cookie as a spoon.

2¼ cups (270 grams) confectioners' sugar

3½ cups (266 grams) unsweetened desiccated coconut

2 tablespoons (28 grams) unsalted butter, melted

5 large eggs

Preheat the oven to 325°F (160°C). Spray a baking sheet with nonstick cooking spray or use a nonstick silicone baking mat. Have a rolling pin at hand.

In the bowl of a stand mixer fitted with the paddle attachment, mix together the confectioners' sugar and coconut on low speed until combined. Add the melted butter and mix until combined. Add the eggs one at a time, waiting until each is fully incorporated before adding the next, and mix until completely combined.

Spoon about 2 teaspoons of the tuile batter onto the baking sheet and, using the back of the spoon, spread it into a 3-inch round. Repeat until the baking sheet is full, leaving about 2 inches between the tuiles. Bake for 10 to 12 minutes, or until the tuiles are golden brown around the edges. Using a metal spatula, immediately remove one tuile from the sheet and drape it over the rolling pin. Let it set and cool, about 20 seconds, before removing from the rolling pin and transferring to a cooling rack. Repeat with the remaining tuiles. If they become too difficult to remove from the baking sheet, return them to the oven for 30 seconds to make them more pliable. Repeat with the remaining batter. Store the tuiles in an airtight container in a cool, dry place for up to 1 week.

Almond Tuiles

MAKES ABOUT 100 TUILES

The lacy dough of these tuiles supports an addition of sliced almonds, which add extra crunch to the cookies. It's a simple dough with few ingredients, so it's a good introduction to making tuiles if you've never made them before.

¾ cup (100 grams) all-purpose flour

1⅓ cups (160 grams) confectioners' sugar

4 large egg whites, at room temperature

7 tablespoons (100 grams) unsalted butter, melted

¾ cup (65 grams) sliced almonds

In the bowl of a stand mixer fitted with the paddle attachment, mix together the flour and confectioners' sugar on low speed until combined. Add the egg whites and mix until smooth, then add the melted butter and mix until everything is combined. Transfer to an airtight container and refrigerate for about 1 hour, or until the batter is chilled all the way through, stirring a few times to speed up the process.

Preheat the oven to 350°F (175°C). Spray a baking sheet with nonstick cooking spray or use a nonstick silicone baking mat. Have a rolling pin at hand.

Spoon ½ to 1 teaspoon of the tuile batter onto the baking sheet and, using the back of the spoon, spread it into a 3-inch circle. Repeat until the baking sheet is full, leaving about 2 inches between the tuiles. (Bake just a few at a time until you've mastered the shaping method.) Sprinkle some sliced almonds on top of each tuile and bake for 3 to 5 minutes, or until the tuiles turn light golden brown around the edges. Using a metal spatula, immediately remove one tuile from the sheet and drape it over the rolling pin. Let it set and cool, about 20 seconds, before removing from the rolling pin and transferring to a cooling rack. Repeat with the remaining tuiles. If they become too difficult to remove from the baking sheet, return them to the oven for 30 seconds to make them more pliable. Repeat with the remaining batter. Store the tuiles in an airtight container in a cool, dry place for up to 1 week.

Cocoa Nib Tuiles

MAKES 75 TO 100 TUILES, DEPENDING ON THEIR SIZE

These tuiles get their crunch not only from their caramelized, lacy texture, but also from the cocoa nibs mixed into the batter. Cocoa nibs are broken-up pieces of cacao beans; they have a complex, almost bitter flavor. They are available in specialty grocery stores and online (see Resources, page 266). If you prefer, you can use finely chopped almonds instead for a similar effect. Serve these instead of chocolates at the end of a meal along with coffee. I also like to dip them in melted chocolate; let it firm up for about 30 minutes before serving or storing. Since there is no flour in the batter, it will spread during baking and needs to be contained. Larger financier-style silicone molds that are 2 to 3 inches in diameter and about 1 inch deep work well for these tuiles, as do regular-size muffin pans; spray those with cooking spray and wait until they are cold to unmold. You can also use bottomless pastry rings; arrange them on a baking sheet and fill them with the batter. These tuiles are very crunchy and very fragile.

3 tablespoons (50 grams) light corn syrup

¾ cup (150 grams) graunlated sugar

9 tablespoons (125 grams) unsalted butter

3 tablespoons (45 grams) heavy cream

1½ cups (180 grams) cocoa nibs

In a medium saucepan over medium-high heat, bring the corn syrup and sugar to a boil, whisking to combine them as the sugar melts. Add the butter and the cream and return to a boil. Whisk well to emulsify, then remove from the heat and stir in the cocoa nibs. Let the mixture cool for 20 minutes.

Preheat the oven to 375°F (190°C) and arrange a silicone mold with 2-inch round cavities on a baking sheet.

Stir the tuile batter to make sure the ingredients are evenly combined. Spoon ¾ teaspoon of the batter into each mold cavity and smooth it flat with a spatula or spoon. Bake for 8 to 10 minutes, or until the tuiles have crisped up. Unmold them when they are still a bit warm (but not so much that you burn yourself or that they lose their shape); if you let them cool fully, they will crack when you try to push them out of the molds. Once out of the mold, let the tuiles cool fully on the baking sheet or a cooling rack, then store them in an airtight container in a cool, dry place for up to 1 week.

Orange Tuiles

The batter of these tuiles is flavored with a lot of orange juice—freshly squeezed, please! Pair them with vanilla ice cream to evoke a Creamsicle, especially if you shape them into cones or bowls and serve the ice cream directly in the tuiles. The batter will keep, covered and refrigerated, for up to 2 weeks, so you can prepare it and then bake the tuiles when you're ready. For perfect circles, you can make a stencil for the batter by cutting a 3-inch circle in the top of a disposable plastic container lid. Drop a small amount of the batter into the stencil and spread it using a large metal spatula, then move the stencil and repeat. The tuiles spread, so don't bake more than five on a baking sheet. To make cones, shape them over a piece of wood or anything you might own that is shaped like a cone, such as a large pastry tip. Shape bowls by pushing the tuiles into the cavities of a regular-size muffin pan and pressing them down on all sides.

---

7 tablespoons (100 grams) unsalted butter, at room temperature

½ cup minus 2 teaspoons (100 grams) packed light brown sugar

½ cup (100 grams) granulated sugar

¾ cup (100 grams) all-purpose flour

⅓ cup plus 1 tablespoon (100 grams) freshly squeezed orange juice

Finely grated zest of 2 oranges (about 2 tablespoons or 25 grams)

In the bowl of a stand mixer fitted with the paddle attachment, beat the butter, brown sugar, and granulated sugar together on low speed until the mixture becomes pale and fluffy. Add the flour and mix until smooth. With the mixer running, slowly pour the orange juice down the side of the bowl. Add the orange zest and mix until everything is well combined. Transfer the batter to an airtight container and refrigerate for a few hours, or preferably overnight, until the batter is chilled all the way through.

Preheat the oven to 350°F (175°C). Spray a baking sheet with nonstick cooking spray or use a nonstick silicone baking mat. Have a rolling pin at hand.

Spoon about ¾ teaspoon of the tuile batter onto the baking sheet and, using a large metal spatula or the back of the spoon, spread it into a 3½-inch circle (or to fill the stencil, if using; see note). Repeat until the baking sheet is full, leaving about 2 inches between the tuiles. Bake for 5 to 10 minutes, or until the tuiles turn light golden brown around the edges. Using a metal spatula, immediately remove one tuile from the sheet and drape it over the rolling pin. Let it set and cool, about 20 seconds, before removing from the rolling pin and transferring to a cooling rack. Repeat with the remaining tuiles. If they become too difficult to remove from the baking sheet, return them to the oven for 30 seconds to make them more pliable. Repeat with the remaining batter. Store the tuiles in an airtight container in a cool, dry place for up to 1 week.

Florentine Bars

Traditional florentines have a characteristic chewy consistency that is due to their high sugar content—here honey and confectioners' sugar—and are usually laced with nuts and candied fruits. My recipe for making florentines in bars saves you the hassle of shaping individual cookies. They make great on-the-go snacks or afternoon treats. I omit the traditional candied fruits in these bars, but you could add some chopped candied orange peel (see page 120), if you'd like.

CRUST

Sweet Dough (page 101)

FILLING

⅓ cup minus 1 teaspoon (90 grams) honey

10½ tablespoons (150 grams) unsalted butter

⅓ cup plus 2 teaspoons (90 grams) water

2½ cups (300 grams) confectioners' sugar

½ cup (60 grams) all-purpose flour

1¾ cups (150 grams) sliced almonds

1¼ cups (150 grams) pistachios, coarsely chopped

MAKE THE CRUST: Fit the Sweet Dough into a 9-by-13-inch glass baking dish and parbake as described on page 101. Let the shell cool completely in the baking dish.

MAKE THE FILLING: If you prepared the crust ahead of time, preheat the oven to 350°F (175°C).

In a small saucepan over medium-high heat, melt the honey, butter, and water.

In a separate bowl, use a spatula to stir together the confectioners' sugar, flour, almonds, and pistachios. Pour the hot honey mixture over the dry ingredients and stir until fully combined. Work fast, since it will set up quickly.

Pour the florentine filling on top of the parbaked shell and use a silicone spatula to spread it as evenly as possible. Bake for about 20 minutes, checking after 15 minutes and then at 5-minute intervals, until the filling has turned golden. Remove from the oven and let cool completely in the pan.

When cool, transfer the whole cookie to a cutting board. The sides will likely be a bit uneven, so trim about ½ inch from each side. You should have a rectangle of about 8 by 12 inches. Cut the cookies into 1-by-2-inch bars. Store the bars in an airtight container in a cool, dry place for up to 3 days, placing a sheet of parchment or waxed paper between each layer to keep them from sticking.

Sesame Florentines

I love snacking on packaged Middle Eastern sesame bars, which are very hard and crunchy. These florentines are much chewier, but their sesame flavor reminds me of those. They are great with a cup of black tea. Don't worry if the batter is not perfectly flat at the bottom of the muffin cups. It will liquefy and even out on its own while baking.

3½ tablespoons (50 grams) unsalted butter

1 tablespoon (20 grams) honey

¼ cup (50 grams) granulated sugar

½ cup (50 grams) sliced almonds, coarsely chopped

2 tablespoons (25 grams) sesame seeds

Preheat the oven to 375°F (190°C) and heavily spray two mini muffin pans with nonstick cooking spray.

In a medium saucepan over medium heat, melt the butter and honey. Remove from the heat and stir in the sugar, almonds, and sesame seeds. Spoon about 1 teaspoon of the mixture into each mini muffin cup. Bake for about 15 minutes, or until the florentines turn light golden brown.

Remove from the oven, and let cool slightly. Place a sheet of waxed paper on your work surface. While the pan is still warm but the florentines have begun to firm up, turn the pan over and tap the bottom so that the florentines fall onto the waxed paper. If you wait too long and have trouble removing them, place the pan back in the oven for about 1 minute, just enough to warm up the pan and soften the cookies. Let the florentines cool completely on a cooling rack, then store them in an airtight container in a cool, dry place for up to 2 weeks, placing waxed or parchment paper between the layers to keep the florentines from sticking to one another.

Macarons & Meringues

In recent years, macarons have become the emblematic French cookie in America, attracting admirers with their beautiful colors just as much as with the wide range of flavors in which they are made. I sell hundreds of them at my patisseries and bakeries every day and love playing with them to come up with new flavor combinations. They are meringue-based but include almond flour (or even matzo meal, in the case of the recipe on page 169), which gives them chewiness as well as an overall more structured texture. Meringue cookies, on the other hand, only include sugar and egg whites (along with flavoring agents, from cocoa powder to grated citrus peel) and are more crumbly—once you break into the beautiful shiny crust of a meringue, it will crumble into pieces on your plate and melt in your mouth. Pastry shops throughout Europe sell meringues in bags or bulk, but it's not a tradition I have observed much in the United States—yet.

Mini Parisian Macarons

Typical macarons are often 1½ inches in diameter, or even as big as 3 inches. I like making mini ¾-inch ones, which makes them most suited to being part of a cookie platter. You should make the filling before you bake the macaron shells so that it has time to cool down and thicken to a pipable consistency, but because you should also remember to age the egg whites, I decided to give you the shell recipe first. I've started with a recipe for a "plain" almond shell, followed by several of my favorite variations.

MACARON SHELLS

¾ cup (75 grams) almond flour

1 cup plus 1 tablespoon (130 grams) confectioners' sugar

3 large egg whites, aged (see note, page 164)

Pinch of cream of tartar

2 tablespoons (25 grams) granulated sugar

ASSEMBLY

Fruit Ganache (page 166) or "Dry" Ganache (page 167), for filling

MAKE THE SHELLS: Line a baking sheet with a silicone baking mat.

In a large bowl, stir together the almond flour, confectioners' sugar, and one of the egg whites until the mixture is smooth. You will have to stir vigorously to get rid of any clumps that might form.

In the bowl of a stand mixer fitted with the whisk attachment, whisk the remaining 2 egg whites and the cream of tartar on medium-low speed until they begin to form stiff peaks. Once they do, sprinkle the granulated sugar little by little over the egg whites, and whip until the peaks are completely stiff. (To ensure you have reached stiff peaks, stop the mixer and lift the whisk from the bowl; if the peaks that form stay pointed, the whites are ready.) Remove the bowl from the mixer and, with a silicone spatula, fold the beaten egg whites into the almond flour mixture, doing so in two stages. The batter should have a pipable consistency but not be too fluffy. If, as you stir it, the batter makes peaks when it falls back into the bowl, continue stirring it until the batter is smooth and flows back in one fluid movement into the bowl.

> MINI ALMOND, PISTACHIO, ROSE WATER, AND BLUEBERRY MACARONS

With a spatula, transfer the mixture to a pastry bag fitted with a ½-inch round pastry tip. You can also just cut a ½-inch opening into the tip of the pastry bag. Pipe the batter into nickel-size mounds, then drop the baking sheet from about 6 inches off the counter to remove any extra air in the batter. Leave the extra batter in the pastry bag or in the bowl, covered with plastic wrap directly on its surface. Let the piped macarons sit at room temperature, uncovered, for at least 20 to 30 minutes. This allows them to form a slight skin that will help ensure a crisp crust and chewy inside. Once the skin is formed, the top of the macarons should not feel tacky. If your kitchen is very hot or the environment is humid, it might take closer to 1 hour.

While the macarons are drying, preheat the oven to 400°F (210°C).

Set the baking sheet with the macarons on top of a second baking sheet and place them in the oven. Bake for 3 minutes, then lower the temperature to 340°F (170°C) and continue to bake for an additional 5 to 6 minutes. Remove them from the oven and let them cool completely on the baking sheet. Once cool, turn the silicone baking mat over so that you can gently pull on it if needed, and delicately remove the macarons.

ASSEMBLE THE MACARONS: Match the macaron shells in pairs that are similar in size.

With a spatula, transfer the filling to a pastry bag fitted with a ¼-inch round pastry tip. You can also just cut a ¼-inch opening into the tip of the pastry bag. Pipe a ½-inch-thick dollop of filling at the center of half of the macaron shells. Press the matching shells onto the filling, twisting slightly so that the two halves stick together. Store the macarons in an airtight container in the refrigerator for up to 3 days, letting them come back to room temperature before serving. If possible (and I encourage you to do it), wait a day before serving them, so that the filling can soften the inside of the shells and make for a moist macaron.

< MINI ROSE WATER, BLUEBERRY, AND PISTACHIO MACARONS

TIPS FOR MACARONS

Macarons are best made with egg whites that have been aged. Pour the whites into a small bowl, whisk them to break them up, then cover the top of the bowl with plastic wrap. Poke holes in the plastic to let the air circulate, and let whites sit in the refrigerator for up to 4 days. Take them out of the refrigerator 2 hours before baking to bring them to room temperature. However, any aging is better than no aging, so if you are pressed for time, let them sit at room temperature for a few hours before baking.

The process of working the batter to remove extra air, called macaronner, ensures that it does not form peaks when you pipe it and is essential to creating a macaron that has a crisp shell and a chewy and moist inside.

I used to use a lot of buttercreams as macaron fillings, but, in addition to being more old-fashioned, in warm weather buttercream has a tendency to soften and melt. By contrast, white chocolate ganache, even with a fruit addition, keeps a perfect consistency. Most of the time people won't taste the chocolate, but the cocoa butter provides a great consistency that is more weather resistant. I use liquid food colorings to add color to the shells; just make sure not to add too much, or it will affect the texture of the finished cookie.

> BLUEBERRY MACARONS

Fruit Ganache

Use this recipe when flavoring your ganache with fruit purees, which you can find in gourmet grocery stores or online. Fruit puree is 90 percent fruit and 10 percent sugar, uncooked, while jam is 40 percent fruit and 60 percent sugar most of the time and is cooked, so it has a completely different texture. You can buy frozen purees (see Resources, page 266), or puree uncooked fruits with 10 percent of their weight in sugar in a food processor. Pass through a fine-mesh strainer until the puree is smooth but not liquid.

2 ounces (62 grams) white chocolate, chopped

¼ cup plus 1 teaspoon (56 grams) granulated sugar

1 heaping tablespoon (10 grams) cornstarch

2 tablespoons (30 grams) heavy cream

7 tablespoons (100 grams) fruit puree

5½ tablespoons (75 grams) unsalted butter, softened

Place the white chocolate in a medium bowl. Whisk together the sugar and cornstarch, which will keep the cornstarch from forming clumps when it is cooked.

In a medium saucepan, bring the cream and fruit puree to a boil, whisking frequently so that the puree doesn't stick to the bottom of the pan and burn. Whisk the sugar-cornstarch mixture into the cream and return to a boil, cooking until the mixture has thickened, 2 to 3 minutes. Pour the mixture over the white chocolate, let it sit for a few seconds, and then whisk until the white chocolate is melted and the mixture is smooth. Whisk in the butter until the ganache is perfectly smooth. Place a piece of plastic wrap directly over the top of the ganache to prevent a skin from forming and refrigerate until it is cold, thickened, and has a pipable consistency, about 1 hour, stirring every 15 minutes or so.

"Dry" Ganache

Use this recipe when flavoring your ganache with extracts (such as coffee) or nut pastes (such as pistachio or hazelnut), which are dryer than fruit purees, and for flavoring agents that have less liquid.

2 ounces (62 grams) white chocolate, chopped

¼ cup plus 1 teaspoon (56 grams) granulated sugar

1 heaping tablespoon (10 grams) cornstarch

½ cup plus 1 tablespoon (140 grams) heavy cream

1½ tablespoons (20 grams) nut paste of your choice (optional)

5½ tablespoons (75 grams) unsalted butter, softened

1 tablespoon (15 grams) extract of your choice (optional)

Place the white chocolate in a medium bowl. Whisk together the sugar and cornstarch, which will keep the cornstarch from forming clumps when it is cooked.

In a medium saucepan, bring the cream and nut paste, if using, to a boil, whisking frequently so that the paste doesn't stick to the bottom of the pan and burn. Whisk the sugar-cornstarch mixture into the cream and return to a boil, cooking until thickened, 2 to 3 minutes. Pour the mixture over the white chocolate, let it sit for a few seconds, and then whisk until the white chocolate is melted and the mixture is smooth. Whisk in the butter and the extract, if using, until the ganache is perfectly smooth. Place a piece of plastic wrap directly over the top of the ganache to prevent a skin from forming and refrigerate until it is cold, thickened, and has a pipable consistency, about 1 hour, stirring every 15 minutes or so.

Pistachio Macarons

Shells: Add a few drops of green food coloring to the egg whites when beating them to stiff peaks.

Filling: Use the "Dry" Ganache filling, adding 1½ tablespoons (20 grams) pistachio paste to the cream when you bring it to a boil.

Rose Water Macarons

Shells: Add a few drops of pink food coloring to the egg whites when beating them to stiff peaks.

Filling: Use the "Dry" Ganache filling, adding 1 tablespoon (15 grams) rose water and a drop of pink food coloring (just enough to give a pale pink color) when you whisk the butter into the white chocolate mixture.

Blueberry Macarons

Shells: Add a few drops of purple food coloring to the egg whites when beating them to stiff peaks.

Filling: Use the Fruit Ganache filling, adding 7 tablespoons (100 grams) blueberry puree to the cream when you bring it to a boil.

Matzo Meal Macarons

MAKES 30 TO 40 SANDWICH COOKIES

I sell these macarons at my pastry shops during Passover. Although they are not kosher for Passover, I like finding new uses for matzo meal that allow me to play with some of the items I make otherwise; you might try making these to use up what's left in your pantry after the holiday. These macarons look just like traditional Parisian ones and follow the same procedure, but they are drier, so they need to sit with the filling in the refrigerator for 48 hours to rehydrate and become moist before you serve them. I include a caramel ganache filling here (which should be made a day ahead), but you can use anything you'd like instead—such as the Fruit Ganache on page 166 or "Dry" Ganache on page 167. You'll have plenty of caramel left over; drizzle it over ice cream or yogurt or over a slice of cake.

FILLING

2 sheets (4 grams) gelatin

½ cup plus 2 tablespoons (125 grams) granulated sugar

3 tablespoons plus 2 teaspoons (62 grams) light corn syrup

1 cup plus 2 teaspoons (250 grams) heavy cream

½ teaspoon (2 grams) fleur de sel

5½ tablespoons (75 grams) unsalted butter, cut into small cubes

MACARON SHELLS

⅓ cup plus 1 tablespoon (37 grams) almond flour

(continued)

MAKE THE FILLING: In a small bowl, cover the gelatin with cold water and let it rehydrate, about 5 minutes. Squeeze hard to remove the water from the gelatin before adding to the recipe.

With a candy thermometer handy, place the granulated sugar and corn syrup in a medium pan and bring to a boil over medium-high heat. Slowly mix in the cream and salt, being careful not to let the mixture splatter or it might burn you. Once the mixture reaches a temperature of 104°F (40°C), stir in the butter. When it reaches 140°F (60°C), stir in the gelatin, and continue to cook until the caramel reaches a temperature of 221°F (105°C). Transfer to a bowl, cover with plastic wrap directly on the surface to prevent a skin from forming, and refrigerate the caramel overnight to let it set.

1/3 cup plus 1 tablespoon (37 grams) matzo meal

1 cup (130 grams) confectioners' sugar

3 large egg whites, aged (see page 164)

Pinch of cream of tartar

2 tablespoons (25 grams) granulated sugar

MAKE THE MACARON SHELLS: Line a baking sheet with a silicone baking mat.

In a large bowl, stir together the almond flour, matzo meal, confectioners' sugar, and one of the egg whites until the mixture is smooth. You will have to stir vigorously to get rid of any clumps that might form.

In the bowl of a stand mixer fitted with the whisk attachment, whisk the remaining 2 egg whites and the cream of tartar on medium-low speed until they begin to form stiff peaks. Once they do, sprinkle the granulated sugar little by little over the egg whites, and whip until the peaks are completely stiff. (To ensure you have reached stiff peaks, stop the mixer and lift the whisk from the bowl; if the peaks that form stay pointed, the whites are ready.) Remove the bowl from the mixer and, with a silicone spatula, fold the beaten egg whites into the almond flour mixture, doing so in two stages. The batter should have a pipable consistency but not be too fluffy. If, as you stir it, the batter makes peaks when it falls back into the bowl, continue stirring it until the batter is smooth and flows back in one fluid movement into the bowl.

With a spatula, transfer the batter to a pastry bag fitted with a 1/2-inch round pastry tip. You can also just cut a 1/2-inch opening into the tip of the pastry bag. Pipe the batter into 1-inch mounds, then drop the baking sheet from about 6 inches off the counter to remove any extra air in the batter. Leave the extra batter in the pastry bag or in the bowl, covered with plastic wrap directly on its surface. Let the piped macarons sit at room temperature, uncovered, for at least 20 to 30 minutes. This allows them to form a slight skin that will help ensure a crisp crust and chewy inside. When the skin is formed, the top of the macarons should not feel tacky. If your kitchen is very hot or the environment is humid, it might take closer to 1 hour.

While the macarons are drying, preheat the oven to 400°F (210°C).

Set the baking sheet with the macarons on top of a second baking sheet, and place them in the oven. Bake for 3 minutes, then lower the temperature to 340°F (170°C) and continue to bake for an additional 5 to 6 minutes. Remove them from the oven and let them cool completely on the baking sheet. Once cool, turn the silicone baking mat over so that you can gently pull on it if needed, and delicately remove the macarons.

ASSEMBLE THE MACARONS: Match the macaron shells in pairs that are similar in size.

With a spatula, transfer the filling to a pastry bag fitted with a ¼-inch round pastry tip. You can also just cut a ¼-inch opening into the tip of the pastry bag. Pipe a ½-inch-thick amount of filling at the center of half of the macaron shells, in a circular shape that doesn't go all the way to the edges. Press the matching shells onto the filling, twisting slightly so that the two halves stick together. Refrigerate the macarons in an airtight container for 24 to 48 hours before serving (48 hours is ideal so that they are perfectly moist). Store them in an airtight container in the refrigerator for up to 3 days longer, letting them come back to room temperature before serving.

Macarons Hollandais (Broken Macarons)

MAKES ABOUT 30 SANDWICH COOKIES

These macarons are the opposite of the Parisian ones on page 160, for which you want the smoothest possible shell. Here, the point is for the shell to crack open when you bake it. The resulting cookies are soft and chewy, and moist enough to stick together and form a sandwich without any added filling.

1 cup plus 1 tablespoon (100 grams) almond flour

1 cup (200 grams) granulated sugar

3 large egg whites

1 tablespoon plus 1 teaspoon (20 grams) water

⅓ cup (40 grams) confectioners' sugar, sifted

Preheat the oven to 400°F (200°C) and line a baking sheet with parchment paper.

In a food processor, grind together the almond flour, ¾ cup (150 grams) of the granulated sugar, and the egg whites until the mixture is smooth. Transfer to a bowl.

Fill a medium pot one-third full with water and bring it to a gentle simmer over medium heat. Place the remaining ¼ cup (50 grams) granulated sugar and the 1 tablespoon plus 1 teaspoon (20 grams) water in a large bowl that will fit over the pot without the bottom touching the water. Reduce the heat to low and place the bowl over the pot. Whisk until the sugar has dissolved and is hot. Remove from the heat, let cool for 30 seconds to 1 minute, and then pour the sugar mixture over the almond flour mixture. Stir with a silicone spatula until is smooth, then stir in the confectioners' sugar until the mixture is smooth.

With a spatula, transfer the batter to a pastry bag fitted with a ¼-inch round pastry tip. You can also just cut a ¼-inch opening into the tip of the pastry bag. Pipe the batter in quarter-size mounds onto the lined baking sheet. Set the baking sheet with the macarons on a second baking sheet, and place in the oven. Bake for about 15 minutes, or until the tops begin to crack and turn light brown.

Remove them from the oven, immediately lift the edge of the parchment paper, and pour about ¼ cup (60 grams) of water under the paper, to create steam that will make the bottom and inside of the macarons soft and a little sticky. Remove the macarons from the parchment paper. Match the macarons in pairs of equal size, then stick two macaron shells together so that they form a sandwich cookie. Let them cool completely on a cooling rack. Store in an airtight container in a cool, dry place for up to 3 days.

Pine Nut Macarons with Almond Filling

MAKES ABOUT 50 SANDWICH COOKIES

The chewy texture of these macarons seems closer to a gommé (see the recipes on pages 119 to 122) than to a traditional Parisian macaron. This also means that they are less finicky to make and can be baked and stored frozen, wrapped in plastic and stored in an airtight container, for up to a month before you assemble them. For a quick filling, use apricot jam as an alternative to the almond filling here. You could also use fig or raspberry jam or a dry orange marmalade, which will complement the candied orange peel in the macaron shells. Whatever filling you choose, it should not be too runny, or it will cause the shells to slide.

MACARON SHELLS

2½ cups (250 grams) almond flour

2¼ cups (250 grams) granulated sugar

3 large egg whites

½ cup (85 grams) finely chopped candied orange peel (page 120)

1 cup (120 grams) pine nuts

FILLING

6½ ounces (200 grams) almond paste

3 tablespoons (45 grams) whole milk, warmed

MAKE THE MACARON SHELLS: Preheat the oven to 350°F (175°C) and line a baking sheet with a silicone baking mat.

In a food processor, grind together the almond flour, sugar, egg whites, and candied orange peel until the mixture is smooth. With a spatula, transfer the batter to a pastry bag fitted with a ½-inch round pastry tip. You can also just cut a ½-inch opening into the tip of the pastry bag. Keep the pastry bag perpendicular to the baking sheet and hold the bag up ¼ inch from the pan. Squeeze the bag, keeping it in one spot, until you have piped a small dome that is about ¾ inch tall, then release the bag. Place 3 or 4 pine nuts on top of each macaron. To smooth out the tops of the cookies and help the pine nuts stay in place, slightly wet a kitchen towel and wring it out well so that it doesn't drip, then roll it up. Hold one end in each hand, and give the tops of the macarons a good tap with the towel so that they are rounded, with no peaks.

Set the baking sheet with the macarons on a second baking sheet, and place in the oven. Bake for about 15 minutes, or until the macarons turn light golden brown. Remove them from the oven and let them cool completely on the baking sheet. When cool, turn the silicone baking mat over so that you can gently pull on it if needed, and delicately remove the macarons.

MAKE THE FILLING: In a food processor, grind together the almond paste and some of the warm milk until the mixture forms a smooth, creamy paste. Depending on the brand and dryness of the almond paste, you may not need the full 3 tablespoons milk. Start by using 1 tablespoon (15 grams), then slowly drizzle in more until you have a smooth paste that is soft enough to pipe but will hold its shape between two macaron shells.

ASSEMBLE THE MACARONS: Match the macaron shells in pairs that are similar in size.

With a spatula, transfer the filling to a pastry bag fitted with a ¼-inch round pastry tip. You can also just cut a ¼-inch opening into the tip of the pastry bag. Pipe a ½-inch-thick amount of filling at the center of half of the macaron shells, in a circular shape that doesn't go all the way to the edges. Press the matching shells onto the filling, twisting slightly so that the two halves stick together. Store the macarons in an airtight container in a cool, dry place for up to 1 week.

Meringues

MAKES ABOUT 25 LARGE MERINGUES

In most French pastry shops, you will find a pile of large, puffy meringues available for purchase. Kids typically love these because they are large and usually affordable on an allowance. My grandfather used to make meringues in his pastry shop's oven during the midday break between 12 and 3 p.m. He'd turn off the ovens, then let the meringues bake in the residual heat. They make a great and easy dessert when combined with ice cream and homemade whipped cream or chocolate sauce. You can make them plain, or have fun with some of the variations I suggest on page 178. Meringues are often baked at a lower temperature or for less time, but here, keeping them at 200°F until they are completely dry allows the sugars to caramelize, giving the meringues a more complex flavor.

---

5 large egg whites

1¼ cups plus
2 tablespoons (280 grams)
granulated sugar

½ cup (50 grams)
confectioners' sugar

Preheat the oven to 200°F (95°C) and line a baking sheet with parchment paper.

Fill a medium pot halfway full with water and bring it to a boil over medium heat.

Place the egg whites and granulated sugar in the bowl of a stand mixer. Reduce the heat to low and place the bowl over the pot, making sure that it is not touching the water. Whisk continuously, to keep the egg whites from cooking, until the sugar has dissolved and the mixture is hot, 3 to 5 minutes.

Place the bowl in the mixer fitted with the whisk attachment and beat on high speed until the whites hold stiff, glossy peaks and are cool, 8 to 12 minutes. Feel the bottom of the bowl to check. Sift the confectioners' sugar over the mixture and, with a silicone spatula, gently fold it in.

With a spatula, transfer the meringue to a pastry bag fitted with a ¾-inch round or star pastry tip. You can also just cut a ¾-inch opening into the tip of the pastry bag. Dab a little bit of the meringue under each corner of the parchment paper so that it sticks in place, then pipe the meringue onto the lined baking sheet in large rosettes or round domes about 2 inches in diameter. Bake for about 2 hours, until the meringues have dried all the way through. Remove one from the oven and taste it to check that it is done before removing all of them from the oven. Once they are fully dry, remove them from the oven and let them cool completely on the baking sheet or a cooling rack. Store them in an airtight container in a cool, dry place for up to 3 weeks.

Chocolate Meringues

Sift in ¼ cup (25 grams) Dutch-process cocoa powder with the confectioners' sugar.

Nutty Meringues

Fold ½ cup (60 to 75 grams) finely chopped toasted nuts or ½ cup (50 grams) nut flour into the meringue with the confectioners' sugar.

Citrusy Meringues

Finely grate the zest of 1 orange, 1 lime, or 2 lemons (or a mix of all three types) into the confectioners' sugar, whisk the two together, and then fold the flavored confectioners' sugar into the meringue.

Chocolate-Dipped Meringues

Melt about 8 ounces (227 grams) of your preferred chocolate, then dip the meringues either completely or partly into it. Arrange them on a baking sheet lined with waxed paper and let them set for about 30 minutes, or until the chocolate is completely dry and no longer tacky to the touch. Store in a cool, dry place with parchment or waxed paper between each layer.

Meringue Fingers with Peanut Butter–Praline Filling

MAKES ABOUT 50 SANDWICH COOKIES

These meringue cookies are sandwiched with a peanut butter–praline filling—the most Franco-American of combinations! They are delicate and crumbly but will become soggy if stored for too long, so plan on serving them the same day you assemble them (both the meringues and the filling can be made ahead). For extra texture and a slight almond flavor, sprinkle some almond flour over the top of the meringues before baking them.

MERINGUES

3 large egg whites

1 cup minus 1 tablespoon (188 grams) granulated sugar

¼ cup (25 grams) almond flour (optional)

PEANUT BUTTER–PRALINE FILLING

½ cup (125 grams) smooth peanut butter, at room temperature

½ cup (150 grams) praline paste, at room temperature

MAKE THE MERINGUES: Preheat the oven to 300°F (150°C), line a baking sheet with parchment paper, and spray the parchment with nonstick cooking spray.

Fill a medium pot halfway full with water and bring it to a boil over medium heat.

Place the egg whites and sugar in the bowl of a stand mixer. Reduce the heat to low and place the bowl over the pot, making sure that it is not touching the water. Whisk continuously, to keep the egg whites from cooking, until the sugar has dissolved and the mixture is hot, 3 to 5 minutes.

Place the bowl in the mixer fitted with the whisk attachment and beat on high speed until the whites hold stiff, glossy peaks and are cool, 8 to 12 minutes. Feel the bottom of the bowl to check.

With a spatula, transfer the meringue to a pastry bag fitted with a ¼-inch round pastry tip. You can also just cut a ¼-inch opening into the tip of the pastry bag. Pipe the meringue onto the lined baking sheet in strips that are 3 inches long and about ¼ inch wide. Dust the tops with the almond flour, if using, and bake for about 15 minutes, or until the meringues have formed a shell on

the outside and have a marshmallow-like consistency in the center. Remove one and taste it to check that it is done before removing all of them from the oven.

Line a second baking sheet with parchment or waxed paper. Remove the meringues from the oven, immediately lift the edge of the parchment paper they baked on, and pour about ¼ cup (60 grams) of water under the paper, to create steam that will make it easier to remove the meringues. Remove the meringues after 1 minute so that they don't become soggy. Transfer them to the second lined baking sheet and let them cool completely. You can keep the meringues, unfilled, in an airtight container in a cool, dry place for up to 3 days.

MAKE THE FILLING: In a small bowl, stir together the peanut butter and praline paste until they are fully combined into a smooth mixture. Store in an airtight container in a cool, dry place for up to 1 week.

ASSEMBLE THE MERINGUE FINGERS: Match the meringues in pairs of similar size.

With a spatula, transfer the filling to a pastry bag fitted with a ¼-inch round pastry tip. You can also just cut a ¼-inch opening into the tip of the pastry bag. Pipe a ½-inch-thick amount of filling along the center of half of the meringues. Press the matching meringues onto the filling, pushing down very slightly so that the two halves stick together. Serve the same day.

Meringue Kisses

MAKES ABOUT 60 COOKIES

While I call these "kisses," they don't look anything like the chocolates that have a similar name. But even though they are square shaped, they are sweet and enjoyable like kisses, and are equally nice to give to others. They will keep for a month in an airtight container or cellophane bag, so they make great little presents or party favors. This meringue is a Swiss meringue, meaning that the egg whites are heated, which gives the end result a crunchier consistency than using a simpler French meringue. Freezing the batter is unusual for a meringue: Here, it's necessary in order to cut the soft meringue into slices. When they bake, pockets of air created by slicing them provide a crumbly and crunchy texture. The length of time you will need to keep the meringue in the freezer before cutting it depends on how powerful your freezer is, but count on at least an hour.

---

4 large egg whites

4 cups (480 grams) confectioners' sugar

2 tablespoons (30 grams) pure vanilla extract

3½ cups (455 grams) raw almonds, toasted (see page 21)

Line a 10½-by-15-inch or similar-size rimmed baking sheet with parchment paper.

Fill a medium pot halfway with water and bring it to a boil over medium heat.

Place the egg whites, confectioners' sugar, and vanilla in the bowl of a stand mixer. Reduce the heat to low and place the bowl over the pot, making sure that it is not touching the water. Let cook until the sugar has dissolved and the mixture reaches 122°F (50°C) on a candy thermometer, whisking continuously to keep the egg whites from cooking.

Place the bowl in the mixer fitted with the whisk attachment and beat on high speed until the whites hold stiff, glossy peaks and are cool, 8 to 12 minutes. Feel the bottom of the bowl to check. Stir in the toasted almonds.

Dab a little bit of the meringue under each corner of the parchment paper so that it sticks in place, then pour the meringue onto the baking sheet. Place the meringue in the freezer until it is completely chilled through, at least 1 hour or up to overnight.

Line a second baking sheet with parchment paper.

With a sharp knife, neatly cut the meringue into thirds or in half (it will soften quickly, so don't work it all at once). Cut each section into 1½-inch squares. Quickly place the squares on the clean lined baking sheet—it's fine if they slightly lose their shape—and place in the freezer for 1 hour.

Preheat the oven to 300°F (150°C).

Bake the squares for about 35 minutes, or until they turn a light brown color. Start checking at 25 minutes to ensure that they don't overbake. Remove them from the oven, let them cool completely on the baking sheet or a cooling rack, then store in an airtight container in a cool, dry place for up to 1 month.

Minis & Mignardises

These cookies are what I like to serve on a plate at the end of a meal, (with financiers, for example; see page 128) in an assortment that will make my guests feel like they just finished the best dinner of their lives. It's a little touch you'll find in most high-end restaurants (typically brought with coffee or the bill) that adds a lot to hospitality at home and invites some more lingering at the table, so that conversations and good times don't have to end just yet. *Mignon* means "cute" in French, and *mignardises* are cute, tiny treats that come in addition to dessert. These recipes are also great if you need to prepare lots of sweets for a buffet, for example, since many of them are mini cakes that feel like bite-size desserts.

Mini Madeleines

MAKES ABOUT 50 MINI MADELEINES

Other than macarons, I think that madeleines are what first come to mind when people think about French cookies. This soft and moist cookie is a pure delicacy, and in its mini size, it's easy to eat more than one—I speak from experience. In France, the classic way of presenting a madeleine is with its signature domed peak up, which is a sign that the batter was perfect and that they were baked correctly, with the centers rising up in the oven. Oddly enough, in America, I find that madeleines are typically served "shell side" up, and have no peak. I suppose it's a good way to hide the fact that they were not baked just right. I trust that you will proudly serve yours peak up! It is important that this batter rest overnight, to let the flour relax. And make sure to butter and flour the molds, rather than using cooking spray, to ensure those peaks. If you bake these in a large madeleine mold, adjust the baking time to 16 minutes. You will get about 15 large madeleines.

---

3 large eggs

½ cup (100 grams) granulated sugar

1 tablespoon (15 grams) light brown sugar

Finely grated zest of 2 lemons

½ cup plus ⅓ cup (112 grams) all-purpose flour

1 teaspoon (4 grams) baking powder

Pinch of salt

8 tablespoons (112 grams) unsalted butter

2 teaspoons (12 grams) honey

Combine the eggs, granulated sugar, brown sugar, and lemon zest in the bowl of a stand mixer fitted with the whisk attachment. Whisk on medium speed for 10 to 15 minutes, or until the mixture is light and fluffy. If necessary, raise the mixer speed to high for a couple minutes.

While the eggs are in the mixer, sift together the flour, baking powder, and salt over a bowl or a piece of waxed paper.

Combine the butter and honey in a medium saucepan over medium-high heat, and let the butter melt. Stir until the honey is well combined. Remove from the heat and, once the egg mixture is ready, stir about one-tenth of the egg mixture into the butter to lighten it.

With a silicone spatula, gently fold the dry ingredients into the egg mixture in two or three additions. Fold the butter mixture into the batter until it is well combined. Cover and refrigerate the batter at least overnight or for up to 3 days.

Preheat the oven to 425°F (215°C). Brush the molds of two mini madeleine tins with butter, and dust with flour. Line a baking sheet with waxed paper.

With a silicone spatula, gently stir the batter to remove the excess air. Transfer the batter to a pastry bag or resealable plastic bag, and cut a ½-inch opening in the tip or corner of the bag. Pipe just enough of the batter to fill each mold three-quarters full. Bake for about 12 minutes without opening the oven, or the madeleines may deflate. After 12 minutes, check to see if the madeleines are completely baked or if they still feel doughy by very gently pressing on their centers; they should bounce back. If they are not completely baked, bake them for about 2 minutes more. The finished madeleines should be light golden brown around the edges and have a domed peak at the center.

Remove the madeleines from the oven, and immediately unmold them by tapping the tins against the prepared baking sheet. They should fall from the tins onto the baking sheet. Immediately arrange the madeleines shell side down so as not to crush their peaks. Serve immediately, or let the madeleines cool to room temperature.

Mini Cannelés

MAKES ABOUT 40 MINI CANNELÉS

It's easy to become obsessed with cannelés. They have a very unique texture, with a thick and crispy crust and a chewy, almost custardy inside, and an unparalleled flavor, thanks in no small part to a healthy dose of rum in the batter. They are traditionally made in copper molds coated with beeswax, which also contributes to their mystique, since they require specialty equipment. But I've found that they also work well made in silicone molds, which are less expensive and often more convenient, so feel free to use those here instead. They won't be quite as crunchy, but will be close enough. The batter needs to rest overnight so that the flour can relax, so plan ahead, while the finished cannelés are best eaten the day they are made. When you look for cannelé molds, buy the mini size (which are about 1¾ inches wide). If you make them full size, which are two and half to three times bigger, bake them for 60 to 75 minutes. If your mold is too small to bake all of the batter at once, don't worry; it can stay refrigerated for up to a week.

2 tablespoons (28 grams)
unsalted butter

2 cups (480 grams) whole
milk

1¼ cups (250 grams)
granulated sugar

1 cup (125 grams)
all-purpose flour, sifted

1 large egg

3 large egg yolks

3 tablespoons (45 grams)
dark rum, such as Myers's

2 tablespoons (30 grams)
pure vanilla extract

In a medium saucepan over low heat, melt the butter. Add the milk, bring the mixture to a simmer, then turn off the heat.

Whisk together the sugar and flour in a large bowl. Whisk the egg and egg yolks into the sugar mixture, then whisk in the milk mixture until everything is well combined. Strain through a fine-mesh sieve into a bowl and let cool to room temperature. Once cool, whisk in the rum and vanilla, cover, and refrigerate for at least 24 hours or up to 4 days.

Preheat the oven to 375°F (190°C).

If using copper molds, heat them in the oven for about 10 minutes, or until they are hot. This step is not necessary with silicone molds. Liberally grease the molds with butter, cooking spray, or food-grade beeswax, doing so more generously if using copper molds. Arrange the molds on a baking sheet.

Stir the batter and transfer it to a large measuring cup or pitcher, which will make it easier to pour into the molds. Fill the molds three-quarters full, then let the batter rest in the molds for 1 hour at room temperature. This will allow the flour to settle at the bottom so that the cannelés don't rise too much when baking, giving them their cake-like, spongy texture.

Bake for 45 to 55 minutes, or until the cannelés reach a deep golden brown color. Remove the molds from the oven and turn them over onto a wire cooling rack. Let the cannelés cool in the molds upside down on the rack, which keeps them from sinking and becoming dense. When cool, unmold them. Serve immediately, or store them in an airtight container for up to 1 day.

Calissons d'Aix

MAKES ABOUT 50 CALISSONS

Calissons d'Aix are diamond-shaped orange-flavored almond cookies with a royal icing crust that provides a crispy textural counterpoint to the soft filling. They are unusual in that they require no baking. Traditionally the dough is spread on a type of rice paper, but the right type is hard to obtain, and I have found that this slightly simplified version is just as delicious. Likewise, although candied melon is often found in the classic version, it's not an ingredient easily accessible in America, so I've made these without. Spreading the dough on the back of a baking sheet will make it easier to roll and cut and will guide you to shape it into a rectangle. Rather than focusing on shaping a perfect rectangle, however, focus on getting the dough to an even thickness of ¼ inch. You might not end up with perfect diamonds for each calisson, but you can always keep any flawed ones as baker's treats.

DOUGH

½ cup plus 2 teaspoons (160 grams) apricot jam

4⅔ cups (400 grams) sliced almonds

2 cups (200 grams) granulated sugar

¾ cup (100 grams) chopped candied orange peel (page 120)

ROYAL ICING

½ cup plus ⅓ cup (100 grams) confectioners' sugar

1 large egg white

MAKE THE DOUGH: Line an inverted 13-by-18-inch baking sheet with parchment or waxed paper.

In a small saucepan over medium heat, warm the jam until it is hot.

In a food processor, grind together the almonds and granulated sugar until the mixture is smooth. Add the jam and candied orange peel and process until smooth again. Depending on the size and power of your food processor, you might need to divide all the ingredients in half and process them in two increments, since the dough is very thick and can be hard to process.

Spread the dough ¼ inch thick on the lined inverted baking sheet. If you need to, place a second piece of parchment or waxed paper on top and roll it out with a rolling pin, since the dough is thick and sticky. Let the dough cool completely.

MAKE THE ROYAL ICING: In the bowl of a stand mixer fitted with the paddle attachment, beat the confectioners' sugar and egg white together on high speed until the mixture becomes thick and fluffy, about 5 minutes.

ASSEMBLE THE CALISSONS: Spread a thin layer of royal icing over the top of the whole cookie. With a sharp knife, cut it into diamonds that are about 1½ inches long. In between cuts, dip the knife into hot water and wipe off the excess water with a towel, to ensure that you get a clean cut. Let the icing set up fully, then use a small metal spatula to remove each diamond from the parchment or waxed paper. Store in an airtight container in a cool, dry place for up to 1 week, placing waxed paper between each layer to keep the calissons from sticking.

Caramelized Honey Nougats

MAKES ABOUT 50 PIECES

Nougat, which is more of a candy than a cookie and more often than not contains pistachios or other nuts, can range from soft to very crispy. I like it soft and chewy, with a honey flavor. Here, I give you several ways to shape the nougat into individual pieces: small balls (which you could then roll in chopped nuts; these are the easiest to make), slices, or squares or rectangles. To avoid sugar explosions that might burn you, it's best to cook the syrup in a tall-sided pan. The cooled nougat should still be soft to the touch but dry, and should not stick to your finger more than very lightly. Wrap individual pieces in cellophane squares twisted into papillotes; it is time-consuming but looks really nice. Then place those in a bag to offer them as a gift, or in a box to eat at home.

---

1 cup plus 3 tablespoons (240 grams) granulated sugar

½ cup (160 grams) honey

¼ cup (60 grams) water

2 large egg whites

Pinch of cream of tartar

2 teaspoons (10 grams) pure vanilla extract

1¼ cups (160 grams) almonds, toasted (see page 21) and chopped

¾ cup (80 grams) pistachios, toasted (see page 21) and chopped

With a candy thermometer handy, place the sugar, honey, and water in a medium tall-sided saucepan and cook over high heat until the mixture reaches 275°F (135°C).

While the syrup cooks, place the egg whites and cream of tartar in the bowl of a stand mixer fitted with the whisk attachment. As soon as the syrup reaches 230°F (110°C) on the thermometer, start beating the whites on high speed. Ideally, they will reach stiff peaks just as the syrup comes to the right temperature. However, if you're not sure of the timing, it's best to start them a little early and stop them once they reach stiff peaks, since they will hold while the syrup finishes cooking.

Once the syrup reaches 275°F (135°C), slowly drizzle it down the side of the mixer bowl while the mixer is running. Whisk for about 5 minutes, or until the nougat thickens and cools down. Whisk in the vanilla, then remove the bowl from the mixer. Use a silicone spatula to fold in the almonds and pistachios. Touch the nougat with your hand. If it feels a little warm and sticky, let it cool fully in the bowl.

Once the nougat has cooled and is easily workable, rub your hands with a little bit of vegetable oil and roll the nougat into small balls. Or, to make slices, remove half of the nougat from the bowl and roll it into a rope ½ inch thick, then cut the rope into 1½-inch slices. Repeat with the remaining mixture.

Alternatively, to make squares, pour the nougat while it is still slightly warm into a greased 9-inch square baking pan. Let it cool completely in the pan, then transfer to a cutting board, spray a sharp knife with nonstick cooking spray, and cut into squares. Wrap the pieces individually (as described in the headnote opposite) and store at room temperature for up to 3 months. You can also leave the nougat as a rope or bar and cut it piece by piece, which is great to do when you have a dinner party.

Mini Fruitcakes

MAKES ABOUT 24 MINI CAKES

Like the Christmas Balls on page 125, these are another alternative to the typical dense holiday fruitcake, baked in mini muffin pans instead. These small cakes are soft, moist, and filled with an assortment of candied fruits that is entirely up to you: Use orange, citron, grapefruit, ginger, or red and green candied cherries, for example, or really anything that you love. If you have extra, you can also top the mini cakes with more candied fruits just before baking them.

⅓ cup (50 grams) raisins

1 cup (240 grams) dark rum, such as Myers's

2 large eggs, separated

1 teaspoon (5 grams) freshly squeezed lemon juice

7 tablespoons (100 grams) unsalted butter, at room temperature

½ cup plus 1/3 cup (100 grams) confectioners' sugar

½ cup (80 grams) assorted candied fruit, rinsed and drained, cut into small pieces

1 cup plus 1 tablespoon (150 grams) all-purpose flour

1 teaspoon (4 grams) baking powder

In a small bowl, soak the raisins in the rum for 1 to 2 hours. Drain before using and discard the liquid.

Preheat the oven to 375°F (190°C) and line two 24-cup mini muffin pans with paper baking cups or spray them with nonstick cooking spray.

Place the egg whites and lemon juice in the bowl of a stand mixer fitted with the whisk attachment, and whisk on medium speed until stiff peaks form. (To ensure you have reached stiff peaks, stop the mixer and lift the whisk from the bowl; if the peaks that form stay pointed, the whites are ready.)

In a clean bowl of the stand mixer, fitted with the paddle attachment, beat the butter and confectioners' sugar together on low speed until the mixture becomes pale and fluffy. Add the egg yolks and candied fruit and beat until fully combined. Add the flour and baking powder and mix just until everything comes together.

Fold the egg whites into the fruit mixture in two additions. Spoon just enough of the batter to fill the muffin cups three-quarters full. Bake for about 15 minutes, or until the cakes are light golden brown and a toothpick inserted in the center comes out clean. Remove them from the oven, let them cool completely in the pans, then store them in an airtight container in a cool, dry place for up to 3 days.

Mini Coconut Cakes

MAKES 48 MINI CAKES

These mini cakes, which have a soft, spongy texture, are good with tea, but their distinct coconut flavor always transports me somewhere exotic and makes me crave a Dark and Stormy, so feel free to serve them with cocktails too. You can spoon the batter into the molds if you prefer, but it's faster and easier to do a clean job with a piping bag.

9 tablespoons (125 grams) unsalted butter, at room temperature

½ cup plus ⅓ cup (100 grams) confectioners' sugar, plus more for dusting

⅓ cup plus 2 tablespoons (125 grams) light corn syrup

3 large eggs

2¾ cups (200 grams) unsweetened desiccated coconut

½ cup plus 2 tablespoons (150 grams) whole milk

1½ cups plus 2 teaspoons (200 grams) all-purpose flour

1 teaspoon (4 grams) baking powder

Preheat the oven to 375°F (190°C) and line two 24-cup mini muffin pans with paper baking cups or spray them with nonstick cooking spray.

In the bowl of a stand mixer fitted with the paddle attachment, beat the butter and confectioners' sugar together on low speed until the mixture becomes pale and fluffy. Add the corn syrup and mix until smooth, then add the eggs and coconut and beat until fully combined. Add the milk and mix until smooth, then add the flour and baking powder and mix just until everything comes together.

Spoon just enough of the batter to fill the muffin cups three-quarters full. Bake for about 15 minutes, or until the cakes are light golden brown and a toothpick inserted in the center comes out clean. Remove them from the oven, let them cool completely in the pans, then store them in an airtight container in a cool, dry place for up to 3 days. Dust them with confectioners' sugar before serving.

Mini Pains d'Épices

MAKES 40 TO 48 MINI CAKES

Pain d'épice, *sliced, often toasted, and spread with butter or honey, is typically served as an after-school snack in France. In miniature form, it takes on a more sophisticated persona, but you can also bake this recipe in a loaf pan if you want, for 60 to 75 minutes. Don't be put off by the long ingredient list—you probably have most of the ingredients in your baking pantry; if not, they are easily available at any supermarket. Use scissors instead of a knife to cut the dried fruits into small pieces to prevent them from sticking too much. You can bake these cakes in silicone mini muffin molds instead of paper-lined muffin pans, but be sure to spray the molds with nonstick cooking spray so that you can easily remove the cakes. Their long baking time ensures that they caramelize, which keeps the fruits from drying out or burning.*

DRY INGREDIENT MIXTURE

1⅔ cups (215 grams) all-purpose flour

Grated zest of ½ orange

Grated zest of ½ lemon

⅛ teaspoon (0.4 gram) ground cinnamon

⅛ teaspoon (0.4 gram) ground cloves

⅛ teaspoon (0.4 gram) freshly grated nutmeg

Pinch of salt

¼ cup (30 grams) pistachios, chopped

2 tablespoons (11 grams) sliced almonds

2 tablespoons (20 grams) slivered almonds

(continued)

Preheat the oven to 325°F (150°C) and line two 24-cup mini muffin pans with paper baking cups.

MAKE THE DRY INGREDIENT MIXTURE: In a large bowl, stir together all of the ingredients.

MAKE THE WET INGREDIENT MIXTURE: In a medium saucepan over low heat, combine the honey, sugar, rum, star anise, and water and cook until everything is melted and fully combined. Bring the mixture just to a simmer, then turn off the heat and let steep for 5 minutes. Remove the star anise, stir in the golden and dark raisins, then stir in the baking soda. The mixture will foam up.

2 tablespoons (12 grams) pine nuts

3 dried figs, cut into small pieces

3 dates, cut into small pieces

3 prunes, cut into small pieces

3 dried apricots, cut into small pieces

WET INGREDIENT MIXTURE

½ cup plus 1 tablespoon (168 grams) honey

⅓ cup plus 1 tablespoon (75 grams) granulated sugar

1 tablespoon (15 grams) dark rum, such as Myers's

2 whole star anise

½ cup plus ⅓ cup (200 grams) water

2 tablespoons (19 grams) golden raisins

2 tablespoons (19 grams) dark raisins

2 teaspoons (12 grams) baking soda

Pour the wet ingredient mixture over the dry ingredients. With a silicone spatula, mix until everything is just combined. Spoon just enough of the batter to fill the muffin cups two-thirds full. Bake for 30 to 45 minutes, or until the cakes spring back to the touch and a toothpick inserted in the center comes out clean. Remove them from the oven, let them cool completely in the pans, then store them in an airtight container in a cool, dry place for up to 3 days.

Mini Chocolate-Spice Cakes

MAKES ABOUT 50 COOKIES

These small chocolate-spice cookies pack a rich flavor into just a couple of bites. I like serving them at the end of a meal as part of a mignardise platter, a small-size assortment of cookies and treats, since they are just the last taste you want to have before leaving the table. You can bake them on a baking sheet for freeform cookies, as shown, or in mini muffin pans lined with paper cups; press a small amount of dough into each muffin cup. The baking time will be the same.

DOUGH

3 cups (390 grams)
all-purpose flour

1 cup (200 grams)
granulated sugar

4 cups (450 grams)
walnuts, toasted (see
page 21) and chopped

2 cups minus 2
tablespoons (360 grams)
chocolate chips

1 cup (150 grams) chopped
prunes

½ cup (50 grams) Dutch-
process cocoa powder

1 tablespoon (7.5 grams)
ground allspice

2 teaspoons (12 grams)
baking soda

(continued)

MAKE THE DOUGH: Preheat the oven to 350°F (180°C) and line a baking sheet with parchment paper.

In the bowl of a stand mixer fitted with the paddle attachment, mix the flour, granulated sugar, walnuts, chocolate chips, prunes, cocoa powder, allspice, baking soda, and baking powder until evenly combined. Pour in the melted butter and warm milk and continue mixing until the dough is fully combined.

Wet your hands so that the dough doesn't stick, and form the dough into small balls about the size of a quarter. Place them on the baking sheet, leaving about 2 inches between each cookie since they will spread when baking. Bake for 8 to 10 minutes, or until the tops of the cookies feel slightly firm. Remove the cookies from the oven and let them cool completely on the baking sheet.

1 teaspoon (4 grams) baking powder

8 ounces (227 grams) unsalted butter, melted

2 cups (500 grams) whole milk, warmed

GLAZE

2 cups (240 grams) confectioners' sugar

¼ to ½ cup (60 to 120 grams) water, plus more if needed

MAKE THE GLAZE: In a large bowl, whisk together the confectioners' sugar and just enough water to make a smooth glaze that has a pourable consistency. Start with about ¼ cup (60 grams) water, then add more if needed until you reach the desired consistency, adjusting the amount of water for a thicker or thinner icing depending on your personal preference (add it a little at a time to make sure you don't accidentally make it too thin).

Line two baking sheets with waxed paper. Dip the top of each cookie into the glaze, letting the excess run down the sides of the cookie. Let the cookies dry completely on the lined baking sheets at room temperature, 30 to 45 minutes. After they are dry, store them in an airtight container in a cool, dry place for up to 1 week.

Peanut–Chocolate Chip Lollipops

MAKES ABOUT 20 COOKIES

I love chocolate chip cookies, but since you probably already have a favorite recipe, I wanted to give you something fun and new. To make these "lollipops," use Popsicle sticks, sturdy lollipop sticks, heavy-duty skewers, or even pretzel sticks. You can make the cookies with any nuts you'd like, or a mix, or leave them out completely, or add chopped dried fruits. I like to press the chocolate chips into the dough rather than mix them in, but you can do the latter if you prefer. If you want to serve these lollipops as a centerpiece, you can paint or decorate a Styrofoam cone and then insert the cookies on their sticks to make a "cookie tree."

1 large egg yolk

2 tablespoons (30 grams) whole milk

1 cup (80 grams) peanuts, toasted (see page 21) and chopped

½ cup plus ⅓ cup (100 grams) all-purpose flour

¼ cup (50 grams) granulated sugar

Pinch of salt

3½ tablespoons (50 grams) unsalted butter, cut into small cubes

2 cups (400 grams) turbinado sugar, such as Sugar in the Raw

1 cup (190 grams) semisweet chocolate chips

1 cup (190 grams) white chocolate chips

Preheat the oven to 350°F (175°C) and line a baking sheet with parchment paper.

In a small bowl, stir together the egg yolk, milk, and peanuts, and set aside.

Place the flour, granulated sugar, and salt in a large bowl and use your fingertips to combine them. Add the butter and continue using your fingertips to rub it into the flour mixture, breaking it up into pea-size pieces.

Make a well in the center of the bowl by pushing the dry ingredients up its sides. Pour the peanut mixture into the well and, with your fingertips, mix all the ingredients together to form a ball.

Sprinkle half of the turbinado sugar onto your work space and transfer the dough onto it. Press the dough down, sprinkle more turbinado sugar on top, then roll out the dough until it is ½ inch thick. The sugar keeps the dough from sticking and gives the cookies a nice crust. With a 2-inch round cookie cutter, cut the dough into circles and transfer them to the lined baking sheet. Press a few semisweet and white chocolate chips on top of each cookie, then bake for about 15 minutes, or until the edges turn light brown.

Remove them from the oven and immediately insert a Popsicle or lollipop stick into the side of each cookie. Make sure to push it in far enough so that it will not fall out or break the cookie—almost all the way to the other side of the cookie without breaking through. Let the cookies cool completely on the baking sheet.

Once cool, use a metal spatula to remove the cookies from the baking sheet. Package them individually by placing a small cellophane or plastic bag over each one and tying a ribbon around the stick to close the bag, or store them in an airtight container. They will keep in a cool, dry place for up to 1 week.

Oatmeal Lollipops

MAKES 30 TO 40 COOKIES

Oatmeal cookies often have a wholesome air to them, but when made into lollipops, anything serious about them disappears. You can add chocolate chips to the dough if you'd like, or replace the dark raisins with dried currants or cranberries. The dough can be frozen and the cookies baked straight from the freezer.

8 ounces (227 grams) unsalted butter, at room temperature

1⅓ cups (265 grams) granulated sugar

1 large egg

2 tablespoons (40 grams) honey

3 cups (300 grams) rolled oats

½ cup (75 grams) golden raisins

½ cup (75 grams) dark raisins

4 ounces (113 grams) carrots, freshly grated (1 cup)

1 cup (110 grams) walnut pieces

2¼ cups (300 grams) all-purpose flour

2 teaspoons (8 grams) salt

1½ teaspoons (9 grams) baking soda

1½ teaspoons (3 grams) ground cinnamon

Preheat the oven to 375°F (190°C) and line two baking sheets with parchment paper.

In the bowl of a stand mixer fitted with the paddle attachment, beat the butter and sugar together on low speed until the mixture becomes pale and fluffy. Add the egg and honey and mix until just combined, then add the oats, golden and dark raisins, carrots, and walnuts and mix until evenly combined.

In a separate bowl, whisk together by hand the flour, salt, baking soda, and cinnamon. Add the dry ingredients to the butter mixture and mix until everything is evenly combined. With your hands, roll the dough into golf ball–size balls, and place them on the baking sheets, not more than 6 to 8 per sheet since these cookies spread. Bake for about 15 minutes, or until the edges are golden brown but the centers are lighter than that. Be careful not to overbake, or they can become too crispy.

Remove from the oven and immediately insert a Popsicle or lollipop stick into the side of each cookie. Make sure to push it in almost all the way to the other side of the cookie without breaking through. Let the cookies cool completely on the baking sheets.

Once cool, use a metal spatula to remove the cookies from the baking sheets. Package them individually by placing a small cellophane or plastic bag over each one and tying a ribbon around the stick to close the bag, or store them in an airtight container. They will keep in a cool, dry place for up to 1 week.

Italian Cookies

When I moved to New York, I discovered the rich tradition of Italian cookies: Going to Italian pastry shops on Arthur Avenue or in Little Italy was a revelation. I also learned a variety of Italian cookie recipes when I worked at Le Cirque, since owner Sirio Maccioni is fond of them. When they are well made, Italian cookies are truly outstanding, and I love nothing more than sitting at a table with friends and seeing them brought out on a platter. I make several variations of biscotti, including some that only cook once, along with other classics like Pignoli and Venetian Cookies. It's easy to play with the flavors of most of the cookies here, by varying the spices of a biscotti or the filling of the purses, for example, to reflect your own preferences or your family traditions—something very Italian to do.

Double Chocolate Logs

MAKES ABOUT 50 COOKIES

These bite-size cookies are unglazed and very simple to make. They are almost like biscotti, but unlike traditional biscotti, they are only baked once, requiring less work on your end. Because these contain little fat, they are hard and crumbly. Their size makes them perfect for holiday cookie exchanges or as part of an assortment of cookies when full-size biscotti would be too much to eat. The finished cookies can be frozen, well wrapped in plastic and stored in an airtight container, for up to a month.

3½ cups (470 grams) all-purpose flour

1¾ cups (350 grams) granulated sugar

1⅔ cups (240 grams) almonds, toasted (see page 21)

1 cup (190 grams) chocolate chips

1 tablespoon (6 grams) Dutch-process cocoa powder

1 teaspoon (3 grams) ground cinnamon

4 large eggs

½ teaspoon (2.5 grams) pure vanilla extract

Preheat the oven to 375°F (190°C) and line two baking sheets with parchment paper.

In the bowl of a stand mixer fitted with the paddle attachment, mix the flour, sugar, almonds, chocolate chips, cocoa powder, and cinnamon until evenly combined. Add the eggs one at a time, waiting until each is fully incorporated before adding the next. Add the vanilla and mix until everything is fully combined.

Transfer the dough to a lightly floured surface and divide it into four pieces. Roll each piece into a 1½-inch-thick log. Place two logs on each lined baking sheet, and bake for 20 to 30 minutes, or until the tops feel slightly firm.

Remove the logs from the oven and let them cool completely on the baking sheets. Then, using a serrated knife, cut each log on the bias into ½-inch-thick slices. Store them in an airtight container in a cool, dry place for up to 2 weeks, or in the freezer for up to 1 month.

Dark Chocolate–Spiced Nut Biscotti

MAKES ABOUT 50 COOKIES

The rich chocolate flavor of these cookies is deepened by a bit of spice from cinnamon, allspice, and ginger. And if that weren't enough, they are also glazed in chocolate along their length. Biscotto means "cooked twice": The first time the biscotti are baked whole, as a log; and the second time sliced, which dries up the sides of the cookie and makes them extra crunchy. When cutting the biscotti, do it on the bias, which is what gives them their recognizable shape.

DOUGH

8½ tablespoons (120 grams) unsalted butter

2 cups (400 grams) granulated sugar

3 large eggs

3 cups (375 grams) all-purpose flour

½ cup (50 grams) Dutch-process cocoa powder

1 teaspoon (6 grams) baking soda

1 teaspoon (4 grams) baking powder

1 teaspoon (4 grams) salt

¼ teaspoon (0.8 gram) ground cinnamon

¼ teaspoon (0.8 gram) ground allspice

¼ teaspoon (0.8 gram) ground ginger

(continued)

MAKE THE DOUGH: Preheat the oven to 350°F (180°C) and line a baking sheet with parchment paper.

In the bowl of a stand mixer fitted with the paddle attachment, beat the butter and granulated sugar together on low speed until the mixture becomes pale and fluffy. Add the eggs and mix until smooth.

In a separate bowl, whisk together the flour, cocoa powder, baking soda, baking powder, salt, cinnamon, allspice, and ginger until combined.

Add the flour mixture, almonds, and hazelnuts to the butter mixture and mix until everything is just combined.

Transfer the dough to a lightly floured surface. Divide it in half, and roll each half into a long log that is 2 to 3 inches thick. Transfer the logs to the lined baking sheet and bake for 18 to 20 minutes, or until the tops feel slightly firm.

Remove the logs from the oven and lower the temperature to 325°F (160°C). Let the logs cool completely on the baking sheet. Then, using a serrated knife, cut each log on the bias

1 cup (130 grams) almonds, toasted (see page 21) and chopped

1 cup (130 grams) hazelnuts, toasted (see page 21) and chopped

GLAZE

2 cups (240 grams) confectioners' sugar

¼ cup (25 grams) Dutch-process cocoa powder

3 tablespoons (45 grams) water, plus more if needed

1 cup (85 grams) sliced almonds, chopped (optional)

into ½-inch-thick slices. Lay them flat side down on the baking sheet (use a second one if necessary to fit them all) and bake them for 6 to 8 minutes, until the top is crispy. Flip the biscotti and continue baking for another 6 to 8 minutes, until the other side is crisp. Remove the cookies from the oven and transfer them to a cooling rack to let them cool to room temperature.

MAKE THE GLAZE: In a large (4-cup) measuring cup or a large bowl, whisk together the confectioners' sugar and cocoa powder. Add just enough water to make a smooth glaze that has a pourable consistency, starting with about 3 tablespoons (45 grams) and adding it a little at a time to make sure you don't accidentally make it too thin.

Line two baking sheets with waxed paper, then place a rectangular cooling rack over one of them. Stand the biscotti slices on their thin side (not the cut side) on the cooling rack, and pour the glaze over them. Sprinkle with the chopped almonds, if desired. Transfer the glazed biscotti to the other lined baking sheet, and let them dry in a cool, dry place for about 30 minutes. Once the glaze is dry, the biscotti will keep in an airtight container in a cool, dry place for up to 1 week.

Biscotti with Anise Seeds

MAKES ABOUT 50 COOKIES

Anise is a popular flavor in the south of France, where I am from. I think especially of pastis, for example, the anise liqueur that is ubiquitous on terraces throughout the region. Even in New York I love having a glass of it in the evening when I am parched, with just a little bit of pastis and lots of water. These biscotti are my Italian twist on a taste of home.

2½ cups (325 grams) all-purpose flour

2½ cups (500 grams) granulated sugar

2 cups (260 grams) whole almonds, toasted (see page 21)

2 cups (260 grams) whole hazelnuts, toasted (see page 21)

1 tablespoon (10 grams) anise seeds

(continued)

Preheat the oven to 375°F (190°C) and line a baking sheet with parchment paper.

In the bowl of a stand mixer fitted with the paddle attachment, mix the flour, sugar, almonds, hazelnuts, anise seeds, salt, and orange zest until evenly combined. Add the eggs one at a time, waiting until each is fully incorporated before adding the next, and mix until everything is fully incorporated.

Transfer the dough to a lightly floured surface and divide it into four pieces, then roll it into logs that are about 4 inches wide and 1½ inches thick. Transfer the logs to the lined baking sheet and bake for about 30 minutes, or until the tops feel slightly firm.

Pinch of salt

Finely grated zest of
1 orange

5 large eggs

Remove the logs from the oven and lower the temperature to 325°F (160°C). Let the logs cool completely on the baking sheet. Then, using a serrated knife, cut each log on the bias into ½-inch-thick slices. Lay them flat side down on the baking sheet (use a second lined baking sheet if necessary to fit them all) and bake them for 6 to 8 minutes, until the top is crispy. Flip the biscotti and continue to bake for another 6 to 8 minutes, until the other side is crisp. Remove the cookies from the oven and transfer them to a cooling rack to cool to room temperature. Store them in an airtight container in a cool, dry place for up to 2 weeks.

Fig Purses

A lot of Italian cookies, particularly holiday ones, are filled with fig jam or dried figs, since the fruit is so abundant in Italy. I like figs a lot, so it's a traditional flavor I'm happy to adopt as well in my tweak on what is both a classic Italian cookie and a breakfast croissant we make in Las Vegas, with a cream cheese filling. This dough is similar to the Sweet Dough on page 101, but with more baking powder, so that it is more crumbly and will rise a bit, to complement the moisture from the figs and raisins. When assembling the cookies, it is useful to keep a small glass of water by your working area, so that you can wet a finger to press down the fig filling onto the dough. Rather than the pinwheel shapes described and shown here, you can also make small square shapes, almost like raviolis, or any filled shape you like.

SWEET DOUGH

8 ounces (227 grams) unsalted butter, at room temperature

½ cup plus 1 tablespoon (110 grams) granulated sugar

1 large egg

2 large egg yolks

2⅔ cups (340 grams) all-purpose flour

1 teaspoon (4 grams) baking powder

FILLING

2¼ cups (450 grams) granulated sugar

1½ cups (285 grams) water

(continued)

MAKE THE DOUGH: In the bowl of a stand mixer fitted with the paddle attachment, beat the butter and sugar together on low speed until the mixture becomes pale and fluffy. Add the egg and egg yolks one at a time, waiting until each is fully incorporated before adding the next, and mix until fully combined. Add the flour and baking powder and mix until everything is incorporated. Remove the dough from the bowl, wrap it in plastic wrap, and refrigerate until it is chilled all the way through, a few hours or overnight.

MAKE THE FILLING: In a small saucepan, combine the sugar and water and heat over medium heat. Once it comes to a simmer, turn the heat down to low and continue cooking until the sugar has dissolved. Add the figs, raisins, almonds, candied lemon peel, orange zest, and cinnamon, and cook, stirring continuously, until the mixture thickens, 10 to 15 minutes.

Remove the mixture from the heat and pour it onto a rimmed baking sheet. Let it cool to room temperature.

2 cups (300 grams) dried figs, finely chopped

1 cup (150 grams) raisins

¼ cup (37 grams) almonds, toasted (see page 21) and chopped

¼ cup (40 grams) candied lemon peel (see page 120), chopped

1 teaspoon (4 grams) finely grated orange zest

¼ teaspoon (0.8 gram) ground cinnamon

Once the fig mixture has cooled, transfer it to a cutting board. If it feels very sticky, wear kitchen gloves. With a large knife, chop it up to give it a slightly smoother consistency. This will also help the filling reabsorb any juices that might have leaked out.

ASSEMBLE THE COOKIES: Preheat the oven to 350°F (180°C) and line a baking sheet with parchment paper.

Remove the dough from the refrigerator and, on a lightly floured surface, roll it out to a thickness of ⅛ inch. Cut the dough into 3-inch squares and transfer them to the lined baking sheet. With a sharp knife, cut four small slits in each square, going from each corner halfway to the center.

Place about a teaspoon of the fig mixture at the center of each square. Wet a fingertip and press the filling down a little so that it spreads almost to the cut edge and doesn't just sit on the dough. Alternate folding one cut corner toward the center and leaving one open to make a shape that resembles a pinwheel.

Bake for about 12 minutes, or until the cookies begin to turn a light brown color. You can serve them warm or let them cool to room temperature on the baking sheet or a cooling rack. Store them in an airtight container in a cool, dry place for up to 1 week.

Bussolai

MAKES ABOUT 50 COOKIES

Bussolai *are often flavored with anisette, a high-proof anise liqueur with a slight lico-rice taste. Whisking the egg white before adding it makes the dough especially flaky. Traditionally, bussolai can be shaped in rings, ovals, or S shapes. The last is the slightly more unusual type of the three but my favorite; since cookies are often round and I like to serve them in assortments, it's a way to bring variety to the table, literally. They are very hard, so they are perfect to enjoy dunked into grappa. When I do that, I always think about the hotel where I stayed in Tuscany that served me bussolai and grappa together—an idyllic experience.*

2 tablespoons (25 grams) unsalted butter, at room temperature

2 cups (250 grams) confectioners' sugar

1 large egg, separated

4 large egg yolks

2 tablespoons (30 grams) anisette

2 cups (250 grams) all-purpose flour

¼ teaspoon (1 gram) salt

Preheat the oven to 350°F (180°C) and line a baking sheet with parchment paper.

In the bowl of a stand mixer fitted with the paddle attachment, beat the butter and confectioners' sugar together on low speed until the mixture becomes pale and fluffy. Add all 5 egg yolks and the anisette and continue mixing until smooth. Add the flour and continue mixing until fully combined.

In a small bowl, whisk (by hand or with a handheld electric mixer) the egg white and the salt until it reaches medium peaks. Pour the whipped egg white into the bowl of dough, with the mixer still fitted with the paddle attachment, and continue beating on low speed for 2 to 3 minutes, until the dough is perfectly combined.

Transfer the dough to a lightly floured surface and roll it into long ropes ¼ inch thick. Cut the ropes into 3-inch-long strips. Roll both ends of each strip to taper them slightly, and form each piece into an S shape. Transfer the cookies to the baking sheet, and bake for 12 to 15 minutes, or until they start turning a light brown color.

Remove the cookies from the oven and transfer them to a cooling rack. Let them cool completely, then store them in an airtight container in a cool, dry place for up to 1 week.

Mocha Sticks

MAKES ABOUT 50 COOKIES

You can decorate this cookie in two ways: with a whole pecan or walnut half, as pictured, for a more sophisticated appearance, or by dipping them in chopped nuts, which is a bit more rustic but requires less precision and tastes just as good. Likewise, you can melt the chocolate over a double boiler or in the microwave or, if you want a great sheen and snap and enjoy working with chocolate, temper it for a pastry shop-worthy result; see page 18 for tempering instructions.

8 ounces plus 1 tablespoon (240 grams) unsalted butter, at room temperature

¾ cup (150 grams) granulated sugar

1 large egg

1 teaspoon (5 grams) pure vanilla extract

2¼ cups (300 grams) all-purpose flour

2 tablespoons (12 grams) instant coffee powder

½ teaspoon (2 grams) salt

¼ teaspoon (1 gram) baking powder

¼ teaspoon (0.8 gram) ground cinnamon

Finely grated zest of ¼ lemon

8 ounces (227 grams) semisweet chocolate, melted

3 cups (330 grams) walnuts or pecans, kept whole or finely chopped

Preheat the oven to 350°F (180°C) and line a baking sheet with parchment paper.

In the bowl of a stand mixer fitted with the paddle attachment, beat the butter and sugar together on low speed until the mixture becomes pale and fluffy. Add the egg and vanilla and mix until combined.

In a separate bowl, whisk together the flour, instant coffee powder, salt, baking powder, cinnamon, and lemon zest. Add the flour mixture to the butter mixture and mix until everything is just combined.

Transfer the dough to a lightly floured surface, shape it into 1-by-3-inch sticks, and transfer the cookies to the lined baking sheet. Bake for about 10 minutes, or until the cookies just begin to turn light brown on their bottom edges. Remove the cookies from the oven and transfer them to a cooling rack to cool completely.

Line another baking sheet with waxed paper. Have the melted chocolate in one bowl and the chopped nuts, if using, in another. Dip one end of each cookie into the chocolate, and then either dip it into the chopped nuts or place a whole nut half on top of the chocolate. Place each cookie on the lined baking sheet and let the chocolate set fully, about 30 minutes. Store them in an airtight container in a cool, dry place for up to 1 week, or in the freezer for up to 1 month, with a sheet of parchment or waxed paper between each layer.

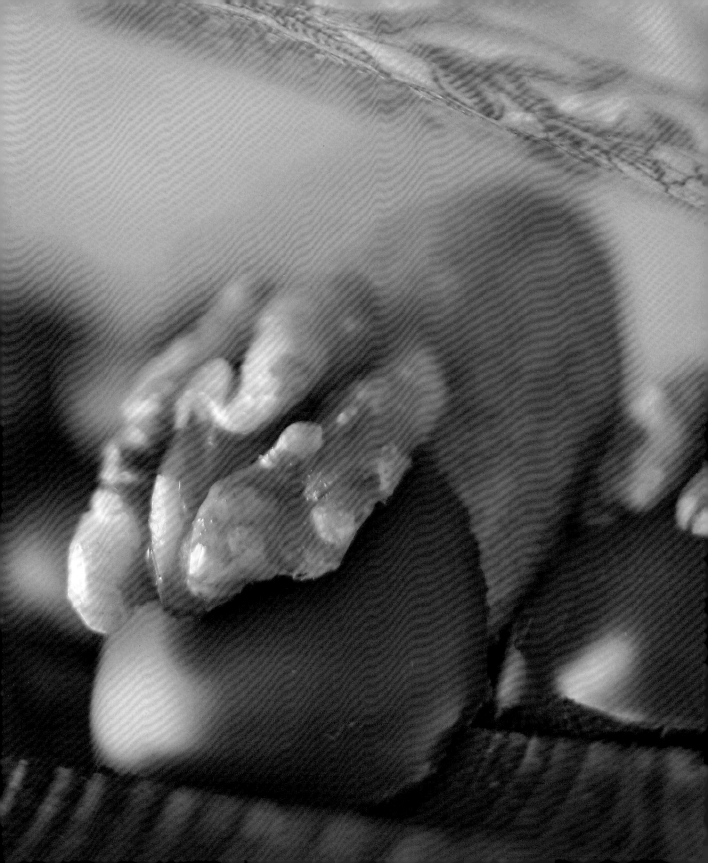

Pignoli Cookies

MAKES ABOUT 50 COOKIES

Pignoli are among the most classic of Italian cookies, and among the ones I love having on hand at all times. These have a crunchy texture that is further accentuated by rolling the unbaked cookies in pine nuts (pignoli in Italian), which then toast during the baking process. The cookies can be frozen for up to a month.

3 cups (360 grams) pine nuts

1 pound (454 grams) almond paste

1 cup (200 grams) granulated sugar

3 large egg whites

1 cup (120 grams) confectioners' sugar

Preheat the oven to 350°F (180°C) and line a baking sheet with parchment paper. Place the pine nuts in a large bowl.

In the bowl of a stand mixer fitted with the paddle attachment, beat the almond paste and granulated sugar until smooth. Add the egg whites and confectioners' sugar, then beat until the mixture is completely smooth. If the almond paste remains too chunky, you can run the dough briefly in the food processor to smooth it out.

Wet your hands so that the dough doesn't stick, and form the dough into small balls about the size of a quarter. Roll each ball in the pine nuts, then place them on the baking sheet, leaving about 2 inches between each cookie, since they will spread when baking, and gently smash them with your hand or the bottom of a glass to flatten them. They should be about 1¼ inches in diameter before baking. Bake for 10 to 12 minutes, or until the cookies turn a light golden brown color. Remove the cookies from the oven and let them cool completely on the baking sheet. Store them in an airtight container in a cool, dry place for up to 2 weeks or in the freezer for up to 1 month.

Traditional Venetian Cookies

MAKES 80 TO 100 COOKIES

You'll see Venetian cookies in every Italian pastry shop, but many don't do them very well—when they are dry, they are not good. When they are well made, they are exquisite cookies, however, with a moist almond paste dough and bright, funky colors. Part of their appeal for me is that brightness, which is so different than anything you'd see in French pastry shops. The almond paste dough has a lovely flavor; it is split into thirds and colored in red and green—along with the third, uncolored, dough, the colors of the Italian flag. The three doughs are then layered with a bit of apricot jam, which acts as glue and adds moisture to the cookie. If your almond paste is stiff, warm it up with your hands and massage it to soften, or grate it with a cheese grater before putting it in the mixer.

DOUGH

1 pound (454 grams) almond paste

2 cups (400 grams) granulated sugar

1½ pounds (680 grams) unsalted butter, at room temperature

8 large eggs, separated

2 teaspoons (10 grams) pure almond extract

4 cups (520 grams) all-purpose flour

½ teaspoon (2 grams) salt

20 to 24 drops green liquid food coloring

16 to 20 drops red liquid food coloring

(continued)

MAKE THE DOUGH: Preheat the oven to 350°F (180°C). Spray three identical 10½-by-15-inch or similar-size rimmed baking sheets with nonstick cooking spray and line them with parchment paper. (If you only own one or two baking sheets, do one or two batches at a time.)

In the bowl of a stand mixer fitted with the paddle attachment, mix the almond paste and sugar to break up the almond paste. When the almond paste has reached a smoother consistency, add the butter and beat on low speed until the mixture becomes pale and fluffy. Add the egg yolks and mix until smooth, then add the almond extract, flour, and salt, and mix until fully combined.

In a separate bowl, whisk the egg whites on medium speed until medium peaks form. With a silicone spatula, fold the egg whites into the almond paste mixture.

Divide the dough evenly among three bowls. (For maximum precision, do this by weight.) Leave one bowl of dough plain white. Add the green food coloring to the second bowl and mix until the dough is evenly colored. Add the red food coloring to

20 ounces (600 grams) apricot preserves

5 ounces (150 grams) semisweet chocolate, chopped

the third bowl and mix until evenly colored. Pour each dough onto a separate lined baking sheet, and spread it as evenly as possible to fill the sheet. Bake for about 12 minutes, or until the cookie layers pull away from the edges of the pan. Let the cookie layers cool completely in the pans.

ASSEMBLE THE COOKIES: While the cookie layers cool, heat the apricot preserves in a medium saucepan over low heat until they reach a slightly loose consistency.

Invert the green cookie layer onto a baking sheet or cutting board covered with waxed paper. This will be the bottom layer. Spread half of the warm preserves onto the green layer, then invert the white layer on top of the green one and spread it with the remaining preserves. Invert the red layer on top of the white one; this will be the top layer of the cookies. Cover the top with plastic wrap, put a baking sheet on top, and add a weight, such as a couple of heavy cans, on top of the baking sheet to press the cookie layers together. Refrigerate the entire setup for about 30 minutes to let the layers set together.

Melt the chocolate in the microwave in 10-second increments, keeping a close eye on it so that it doesn't burn, or over a double boiler, until it reaches a spreadable consistency.

Remove the cookie setup from the refrigerator, remove the baking sheet and plastic wrap, and spread the chocolate evenly over the top. Since you will trim the edges later, no need to worry about the chocolate perfectly covering them. Place the cookies in a cool, dry place until the chocolate begins to set and is no longer sticky to the touch, about 30 minutes. Trim the edges of the cookie to make them even, then cut it into 1-inch squares with a sharp knife, dipping the knife in warm water and wiping it dry in between each cut. Store the cookies in an airtight container in a cool, dry place for up to 1 week, with a sheet of parchment or waxed paper between each layer.

Ricotta Cookies

MAKES ABOUT 50 COOKIES

Since you bought a bottle of anisette to make Bussolai (page 22), I thought I'd give you another reason to use it. This simple cookie is made with fresh whole milk ricotta—buy the best you can find—and glazed with an anisette icing. You can use the cookies as a base to play with other flavors in the glaze if you'd prefer, such as Cointreau, kirsch, or rum. On the nonalcoholic side, use orange blossom water or orange or grapefruit juice and zest.

DOUGH

8 ounces (227 grams) unsalted butter, at room temperature

1 cup (227 grams) fresh whole milk ricotta

1 cup (200 grams) granulated sugar

2 large eggs

2 teaspoons (10 grams) pure vanilla extract

3½ cups (455 grams) all-purpose flour

1 teaspoon (4 grams) baking powder

1 teaspoon (4 grams) salt

GLAZE

1 cup (120 grams) confectioners' sugar

2 to 3 tablespoons (30 to 45 grams) anisette, plus more if needed

MAKE THE DOUGH: Preheat the oven to 350°F (180°C) and line two baking sheets with parchment paper.

In the bowl of a stand mixer fitted with the paddle attachment, mix the butter, ricotta, and granulated sugar until combined. Add the eggs and vanilla and mix until smooth. Add the flour, baking powder, and salt and mix until just combined.

Using a spoon, drop mounds the size of a quarter onto the lined baking sheets. Bake for about 10 minutes, or until the edges just start to turn a light golden brown color. Remove the cookies from the oven and let them cool completely on the baking sheets.

MAKE THE GLAZE: In a large bowl, whisk together the confectioners' sugar and the anisette to make a smooth glaze that has a pourable consistency. If you need to thin the glaze further, add a little more anisette, a little at a time to make sure you don't accidentally make it too thin.

Line two baking sheets with waxed paper. Dip the top of each cookie into the glaze, letting the excess run down the sides of the cookie. Let the cookies dry on the lined baking sheets at room temperature for at least 30 minutes. Once the glaze is dry, the cookies will keep in an airtight container in a cool, dry place for up to 2 weeks, with a sheet of parchment or waxed paper between each layer.

Calendar of Cookies

For many years, Payard Pâtisserie sold cutout cookies decorated with royal icing that changed each month and reflected a seasonal holiday or theme, such as Easter eggs in April, picnic baskets in August, jack-o'-lanterns in October, and ornaments in December. My regular customers loved to come in and discover what we'd come up with. We had a lot of fun with those cookies, but unfortunately it became too time-consuming to continue each year. It's a wonderful tradition to have at home, however; one in which you can involve the whole family. You can bake and decorate any of the three cookie doughs (Sugar, Gingerbread, and Gluten-Free) given on the following pages. They make between 24 and 48 cookies on average, depending on the size of your cookie cutters, which works well for decorating with multiple layers of royal icing: By the time you are done with the first round of colors, the first cookie is dry and you can start piping the rest of the decorations right away. If you are only decorating a few cookies at once, just wait a bit longer between each layer to ensure that everything is dry, about 30 minutes depending on the humidity in the air of the room in which you are decorating them and the time of year; the more humidity, the longer it will take. The layer doesn't need to be completely dry, but dry enough to withstand a second layer without it sliding—the way you would paint walls in a house.

Sugar Cookies

MAKES ABOUT 25 THREE-INCH COOKIES

I use this sugar dough as the base for most of my holiday cookies: It's simple and has a nice vanilla flavor without outshining the star of the show—its richly decorated top.

12 ounces plus
3 tablespoons (375 grams)
unsalted butter, at room
temperature

1½ cups plus
2 tablespoons (200 grams)
confectioners' sugar

½ vanilla bean or
1 teaspoon (5 grams)
pure vanilla extract

1 large egg yolk

3 cups plus 1 tablespoon
(400 grams) all-purpose
flour

Place the butter and confectioners' sugar in the bowl of a stand mixer fitted with the paddle attachment. Split the vanilla bean and scrape the seeds into the bowl (or add the vanilla extract), then beat on medium speed until the mixture is smooth and well incorporated. Add the egg yolk and mix until combined, then add the flour and mix until the dough is well combined. Remove the dough from the bowl, wrap it in plastic wrap, and refrigerate for about 2 hours, or until it is chilled all the way through. You can freeze it for up to 1 month.

Preheat the oven to 375°F (190°C) and line two baking sheets with parchment paper.

Remove the dough from the refrigerator and transfer it to a lightly floured surface. Roll it out until it is ¼ inch thick. Use a 3-inch cookie cutter (in any shape you'd like) to cut the cookies, then transfer them to the baking sheets. You can reroll the scraps of cookie dough to cut out more cookies. Bake for 10 to 12 minutes, or until the bottom edges of the cookies turn a very light golden brown.

Remove the cookies from the oven and let them cool completely on the baking sheets, then store in an airtight container in a cool, dry place for up to 2 weeks.

Gingerbread Cookies

MAKES ABOUT 25 FOUR-INCH COOKIES

The most classic shape for gingerbread cookies is little men and women, of course, but you can cut this dough into any shape you'd like. This dough is also perfect for making ginger-bread houses or Christmas ornaments. For a slightly softer and chewier cookie, bake the dough for slightly less time, and for a harder and crunchier cookie, leave it in the oven a bit longer. A softer cookie will not keep for as long as a harder one and won't sustain being hung as an ornament, however. If you can, refrigerate the dough overnight rather than for just a couple of hours. The resulting cookies will be less dense.

4⅔ cups (600 grams) all-purpose flour

1 teaspoon (6 grams) baking soda

2 tablespoons (12 grams) ground cinnamon

1 tablespoon (6 grams) ground cloves

1 tablespoon (6 grams) ground ginger

15 tablespoons (215 grams) unsalted butter, at room temperature

1 cup plus 1 tablespoon (215 grams) granulated sugar

¾ cup (255 grams) light corn syrup

⅓ cup plus 2 teaspoons (90 grams) whole milk

Line a baking sheet with parchment paper and spray it with nonstick cooking spray.

Sift together the flour, baking soda, cinnamon, cloves, and ginger into the bowl of a stand mixer. Fit the mixer with the paddle attachment, then mix on low speed to fully combine the ingredients.

In a medium saucepan over low heat, melt the butter, then add the sugar, corn syrup, and milk, whisking to combine. Bring the mixture to a boil.

With the mixer on low speed, carefully pour the butter mixture down the side of the bowl, avoiding splatters. Once all the butter mixture has been added, raise the speed of the mixer to medium-high and continue mixing until everything is well combined and the dough is smooth.

Carefully pour the dough onto the prepared baking sheet. (Be careful; it will still be hot.) Place a piece of parchment or waxed paper on top of the dough and use your hands to flatten it as much as possible. Let it cool to room temperature, then cover in plastic wrap and refrigerate until the dough is fully chilled, at least 2 hours but preferably overnight.

Preheat the oven to 375°F (190°C) and line two baking sheets with parchment paper.

Remove the dough from the refrigerator and transfer it to a lightly floured surface. Roll it out until it is ¼ inch thick. Use a 4-inch cookie cutter (in any shape you'd like) to cut the cookies, then transfer them to the baking sheets. You can reroll the scraps of cookie dough to cut out more cookies. Bake for about 15 minutes, or until the bottom edges of the cookies turn a light golden brown.

Remove the cookies from the oven and let them cool completely on the baking sheets, then store them in an airtight container in a cool, dry place for up to 2 weeks.

Gluten-Free Cookies

MAKES ABOUT 42 TWO- TO THREE-INCH COOKIES

I get more and more customers who want to enjoy my pastries and cookies but have celiac disease or can't eat gluten for other reasons. So I've developed this basic cookie dough, which is a great substitute for the regular sugar cookie dough (page 233) or the gingerbread dough (page 234) when you want to make gluten-free holiday cookies. The dough is also great for Passover, since it doesn't include wheat flour.

8 ounces (225 grams) unsalted butter, at room temperature

1 cup (200 grams) granulated sugar

2 large egg yolks

1½ teaspoons (7.5 grams) gluten-free vanilla extract

2¼ cups (290 grams) Gluten-Free Flour Blend (recipe follows)

¼ teaspoon (1 gram) salt

In the bowl of a stand mixer fitted with the paddle attachment, beat the butter and sugar together on low speed until the mixture becomes pale and fluffy. Add the egg yolks and vanilla and continue beating, scraping the bowl often, until well combined. Add the flour blend and salt and beat until everything is well combined.

Remove the dough from the bowl, divide it in half, and wrap each half in plastic wrap. Refrigerate for about 2 hours, or until it is chilled all the way through. You can also freeze the dough, well wrapped in plastic and stored in an airtight container, for up to 1 month.

Preheat the oven to 350°F (175°C) and line two baking sheets with parchment paper.

Lightly sprinkle your work surface with the flour blend, then take out half the dough, leaving the other half refrigerated so that it doesn't get warm and become impossible to roll. Roll out the dough until it is ¼ inch thick. Cut with a 2½-inch cookie cutter (in any shape you'd like), and transfer the cookies to the baking sheets, leaving 1 inch between them. Reroll the scraps and cut out more cookies. Bake for 8 to 12 minutes, or until the edges are light brown. Remove the cookies from the oven, let the cookies sit for 2 minutes on the baking sheets, then transfer them to a cooling rack to cool completely. Store them in an airtight container in a cool, dry place for up to 1 week.

Gluten-Free Flour Blend

MAKES 3 CUPS (400 GRAMS)

2 cups (270 grams) rice flour

²⁄₃ cup (90 grams) potato starch

¹⁄₃ cup (35 grams) tapioca starch

1 teaspoon (2.5 grams) xanthan gum

Whisk together all of the ingredients. Store in an airtight container with a tight-fitting lid for up to 1 month. Whisk again before using.

Royal Icing

MAKES 2 CUPS (350 GRAMS)

This icing can be piped or spread onto baked cookies. You'll want a slightly thinner consistency for the base color of the cookie, so that the icing can spread, and a thicker one for the cookie's outlines and the detail elements. For a thinner consistency, add a little more lemon juice, until you reach the consistency desired. If you are using multiple colors on the same cookie, glaze it with the first layer of royal icing, let the cookies sit for 30 minutes (or up to overnight in the refrigerator, if you want to glaze them ahead of time), then pipe additional colors on top. This will ensure that the base layer of icing is firm enough. Just a note: The icing contains raw egg whites, so it isn't recommended if you need to avoid them for health or safety reasons; alternatively, you can use pasteurized egg whites.

3 cups (360 grams) confectioners' sugar

2 egg whites

2 drops lemon juice

Food coloring (optional)

In the bowl of a stand mixer fitted with the paddle attachment, beat the confectioners' sugar and egg whites for about 5 minutes, until the icing is thick and holds its shape. Add the lemon juice, which will help the icing set quickly, and the food coloring, if using, a little at a time until the perfect color is reached. If you need several small quantities of colored icing, divide it before adding the color, placing each part in a separate bowl, then stir in your chosen colors. Use immediately, or refrigerate in an airtight container for up to 3 days. If you refrigerate the icing, let it come back to room temperature before using, then rewhip it a bit. If it has stiffened, add a drop or two of lemon juice to loosen it. If you let it sit in between frosting batches of cookies, place a damp towel on top of the bowl, without touching the icing; this will keep it moist.

DECORATING WITH ROYAL ICING

Decorating cookies with royal icing is much easier than it looks, which is good news since it means you can create very impressive works with just a little practice. You will typically use two variations of royal icing: a thinner base that you will use to "flood," or cover, the cookie, and a thicker piping icing, which you will use for outlines, to create specific shapes, for detailed decorations, and to add dimension. This thicker icing will need to be placed in a piping bag, which will give you control over the piping. To test that your icing has the right consistency for its intended purpose, dip a spoon in the icing, then hold it at an angle; if it drips, it is ready for flooding; if it holds its shape, it's ready for piping. If your flooding icing is too loose, it will be hard to follow the outline, it will break between the lines, and it will not cover the cookie. If you see too many bubbles, your icing should be stiffer.

There are two ways to flood a cookie with icing. The first is to pipe the outline of the cookie and then fill its inside with the flooding icing, using a toothpick to spread out the icing to the edges. This way is a little bit easier, because you don't have to worry about icing dripping on the sides of the cookie. The second is to use a spatula to spread the flooding icing across the cookie, covering all corners. This method takes a little more skill because you have to be gentle with the spatula so as not to break the cookie, and you also need to make sure to keep the icing on top of the cookie and not on the sides. However, if you are in a rush, the spatula method is much faster. Once the cookie is flooded, let it set for 20 to 30 minutes, or until dry. You can then add decorations and designs on this blank canvas.

Once the base is set, use a piping bag with the smallest possible round tip (a PME #1.5 or Ateco #1 tip is good) to pipe additional layers. (Do not just cut the tip of a pastry bag; that won't be precise enough for decorating.) When using specialty decorations, such as edible pearls or sugars, add these immediately after piping, when the icing is still wet, so that the icing acts as glue and binds the decorations to the cookie.

For a marbleized effect, such as used for the Thanksgiving turkey and leaf cookies (see page 258), pipe the colors one right after the other while they are still wet, without waiting for each color to dry in between layers. Drag the tip of a toothpick through the colors to create a marbled effect.

When you are finished decorating the cookies, let them sit for about 30 minutes to dry completely. Royal icing helps seal in the moisture of the cookies, allowing them to keep longer when stored appropriately. To create party favors, place the cookies in individual cellophane or plastic bags and tie each bag with a ribbon. For a hostess gift, fill a larger bag or a beautiful tin with a few different cookies.

New Year's Eve

I wanted to make something very festive for New Year's Eve, and decided on a crown shape, a symbol of celebration. It also recalls the crown that one receives when finding the favor in the Epiphany *galette* that is typically served in France on Three King's Day, January 6, but sold in pastry shops for several days, if not weeks, earlier. Glaze the cooled cookies with a layer of yellow royal icing, and let set until dry, about 30 minutes. Once the first layer is dry, use white royal icing and a small round pastry tip to pipe the outline and details of the crown to really make the cookie pop. Add a few edible pearls at the crown's tips, and use a very fine pastry tip to pipe "Happy New Year" in the middle of the cookie with white royal icing. Let set until completely dry, about 1 hour, before serving.

Valentine's Day

For Valentine's Day, I always like to create two different kinds of cookies, one a little more feminine than the other, such as one with a bolder color and one with a lighter one. For the hearts shown here, glaze the cooled cookies with soft pink royal icing, and let set until dry, about 30 minutes. Using purple, red, and pink royal icing, in different piping bags fitted with small round pastry tips, draw the outlines of little flowers in a cluster and fill them in with the different colors; let dry. Once dry, outline the flowers with white royal icing using a very fine pastry tip. In the middle of the cookie, write "*Je t'aime*" ("I love you") to give the cookies a romantic French flair, and add some white polka dots. Let set until completely dry, about 1 hour, before serving.

Easter

Use an oval shape to cut out the cookies to look like eggs. You can use any colors you like, but pastels, such as pale yellow, pale pink, pale green, and pale purple, are especially fitting. Glaze the cookies with a base coat of royal icing, and let set until dry, about 30 minutes. Using a piping bag fitted with a thin pastry tip and filled with white royal icing or another complementary color (or multiple colors in separate piping bags), draw patterns of lines and dots across the eggs. Let set until completely dry, about 1 hour, before serving.

Mother's Day

In France, lilies of the valley are often given to moms on Mother's Day, as they mark the season of spring and have a very perfumed aroma. I used a torch-shaped cookie cutter and my fingers to create the shape of these delicate flowers. You can do that, or make any other flower using your desired cutter. Cover the cooled cookies with pale green royal icing, and let set until dry, about 30 minutes. Once dry, use a different shade of green royal icing to draw the stems of the flowers. Let the cookies dry for about 10 minutes, and then, using white royal icing, pipe flowers onto the stems. At the bottom of the stems, draw a little pink bow. Let it set before outlining it with more royal icing and writing "Mom." Let set until completely dry, about 1 hour, before serving.

Father's Day

These cookies are shaped like button-down shirts. At Payard, we make our own cutters, but you can also find similar ones in stores. Glaze the whole cookie with a base of royal icing (here, light yellow), and let set until dry, about 30 minutes. Using a piping bag filled with white royal icing, draw the collar of the shirt; using a smaller tip, draw the outline of the shirt around the edge of the cookie. On the two sides, draw little sleeves folded to the front of the shirt. Piped white stripes and buttons and a Payard monogram are shown here, but feel free to customize the shirt to what your own dad wears; just remember to let each "layer" of icing set before you pipe the next one. Let the cookies set until completely dry, about 1 hour, before serving.

Fourth of July

For Fourth of July and Bastille Day which falls not long after, I always look for ideas that go beyond a red, white, and blue flag. I like making fun shapes, like the ice cream cookies or the little dog pictured here. Dog-shaped cookie cutters can often be found at baking supply stores or online. Cover the whole cookies in white royal icing using a spatula, and let set until dry, about 30 minutes. Using white royal icing, outline the dog to give the cookie a little more dimension, and let set until dry, about 10 minutes. Pipe three red stripes on the dog's stomach, and a little red dot for the nose. Use blue royal icing to pipe the dog's collar: Cut the piping bag a little bigger for the collar, and keep the bag close to the cookie to pipe a straighter line. Pipe a little dot for an eye. Once the collar is dry, draw four stars on top. Let the cookies set until completely dry, about 1 hour, before serving.

Summer Picnic

There are no official holidays in August, but it's a time when everyone likes to relax, so I thought a picnic basket would be perfect. Beach-themed cookies would work well too. To make these, first, glaze the whole cooled cookie in a soft yellow, and let set until dry, about 30 minutes. Once dry, use a dark yellow icing and a very small pastry tip to pipe lines that crisscross the cookies, to look like a wicker basket. On the top, draw a few things with royal icing, such as bread and wine, or anything you'd like to take on a picnic. You can be as detailed as you like, using different colors of icing and very fine pastry tips; remember to let each color of icing set before piping the next one. Let set until completely dry, about 1 hour, before serving.

Rosh Hashanah

To celebrate Rosh Hashanah, the Jewish New Year, I wanted to create a cookie showing apples and honey—foods traditionally eaten to symbolize a sweet year ahead—and thought that a honey jar would be cute. We built the cookie cutter, but you can find some similar ones in specialty shops or online, or you could use separate cutters for the fruit and jar. Start by glazing the bottom of the jar with brown icing, like a classic honey jar, then pipe the small lid in a yellowish brown color. Using dark brown or red royal icing, pipe the outline of the jar and lid. With white royal icing, draw a label on the jar. Once dry, you can pipe an inscription in Hebrew on top of the white label, or any other design you like. On both sides of the jar, add layers of green and red royal icing to create apple slices; let dry, then pipe on details such as leaves and seeds. Let the cookies set until completely dry, about 1 hour, before serving.

Payard

Halloween

For Halloween at Payard, we typically do three different cookies: ghosts, jack-o'-lanterns, and bats. Glaze the cooled cookies with a base coat of royal icing (soft orange for the pumpkins, white for the ghosts, and black for the bats), and let set until dry, about 30 minutes. Once dry, use different colors of royal icing to pipe facial features and other details, letting each color dry before piping the next. Let set until completely dry, about 1 hour, before serving.

Thanksgiving

I typically make two types of cookies for Thanksgiving, one shaped like a turkey and one like a leaf, and give them a unique marbleized effect by piping icing when it is still wet. Prepare a bowl of light orange icing and four piping bags of green, yellow, red, and brown royal icing. For the turkey, glaze the whole cooled cookie with orange royal icing. While the icing is still wet, draw lines down the tail from top to bottom in different colors, then drag the tip of a toothpick or skewer through the lines to create the marbleized effect. Finish with dots of black royal icing. Use silver pearls for the eyes, applying them when the icing is still wet, and red royal icing for the wattle. Let set until completely dry, about 1 hour, before serving.

Hanukkah

A cookie cutter that looks like a glass is easily transformed into the shape of a menorah, but a six-pointed star would be beautiful for this holiday as well. Glaze the cooled cookies in white royal icing, and let set until dry, about 30 minutes. Once dry, outline the menorah with white royal icing and let dry. Use blue icing to pipe nine candles and a few decorative dots, and yellow icing for the flames on top. Let set until completely dry, about 1 hour, before serving.

Christmas

Gingerbread dough is traditional for Christmas cookies, and I usually make ornaments, stars, and snowmen. Decorate them as a family and use them ornaments on your tree or to hang in other areas of your house. To make a hole through which you can pass ribbons, use a very small round or oblong pastry tip to make a small cutout before baking the cookies. The stars are big, beautiful cookies but a little fragile to handle, so keep them on a platter or wrap them in cellophane bags to give as presents; if you are going to wrap them, make sure the icing is completely dry before you do so, or the pearls might fall off. Use white royal icing to define the outline of the cookies and decorate with dots or other details in the middle. Top dots of icing, while they are still wet, with little edible pearls to add some sparkle. Write a name or initial in the middle of each cookie to personalize it. Let set until completely dry, about 1 hour, before serving or packaging.

Acknowledgments

I want to give special thanks to Laurent Tourondel, Philippe Bertineau, Hervé Poussot, Enrique Aranda, Adil Slassi, Nancy Kershner, Eric Estrella, David Carmichael, Lincoln Carson, Michael Mina, Pierre Gatel, Gregory Gourreau, Craig Harzewski, Christopher Hereghty, Johnny Iuzzini, Nicolas Néant, Simon Veuvay, Simon Dupin, Garry Laurdinat, Julien Khalaf, Alex Zamora, and Felipe Coronado. Your talent and friendship continue to inspire me.

A special thanks to Alessandra Altieri Lopez for pre-testing so many of these recipes while working with me at Payard Bistro.

Abby Klausner, my assistant, worked diligently by my side to take care of all the little details needed to make this book, among countless other projects, come together.

Anne McBride, thank you for being so patient and spending hours going through every detail to make this book what it is.

Much thanks to the entire team at Houghton Mifflin Harcourt, who once again worked with me to produce a beautiful book that I am proud of. A special thank you to my diligent and patient editor, Stephanie Fletcher, and thanks to production editor Jamie Selzer.

And to my wife, Fernanda, your constant support enables me to be the best that I can be.

—FRANÇOIS

A huge thank you to François Payard for offering me once again the opportunity to collaborate with you. It's always a tremendous pleasure to learn from you and spend hours debating the finer points of French pastry.

Stephanie Fletcher is an incredibly thorough and attentive editor. She stirred this project with a patience and care that made her a dream to work with.

Kim Kaechele tested recipes with thoroughness, attention to the most minute details, and passion for precision. Thank you for always caring about the difference made by a few grams of butter, and for always going above and beyond the task at hand. Beyond a collaborator, I am thankful for calling you a dear friend.

Thank you to Priscilla Martel and the American Almond Products Company for supplying almond flour for recipe testing.

I am grateful beyond words to my family in Switzerland and to the many friends who tolerated my nearly complete disappearance and yet never failed to ask about the book's progress, in particular Jody Eddy and Maxime Bilet.

As always, the largest share of loving appreciation must go to Ron McBride, without whom nothing I do would be possible.

—ANNE

FRANÇOIS AND EXECUTIVE PASTRY CHEF NICOLAS NÉANT BAKING COOKIES

Resources

Here are a few stores where you'll find ingredients and equipment that might not be readily available in your local supermarkets. However, with the proliferation of supermarkets such as Whole Foods, Wegmans, and Trader Joe's, and the large selection of specialized kitchen equipment now carried by stores such as Target, you should find almost everything rather easily.

Amazon

Use Amazon's extensive selection of kitchenware to buy cookie cutter sets, silicone baking mats, baking sheets, and molds, as well as specialty ingredients.
www.amazon.com

American Almond Products Company

This wholesale company sells nuts and nut flours in 5- and 25-pound boxes.
800-825-6663
www.americanalmond.com

King Arthur Flour

This famed store and mail-order company sells a wide variety of flours and nut flours, as well as pistachio and praline pastes, candied citrus peel, silicone products, and pans and molds.
800-827-6836
www.kingarthurflour.com

L'Epicerie

This amazing online store sells all kinds of hard-to-find pastry (and savory) ingredients in small quantities, such as nut flours and pastes, cocoa nibs, fruit purees, and much more.
866-350-7575
www.lepicerie.com

JB Prince Company

JB Prince is both a store and a mail-order company. They offer a wide selection of equipment for professionals and home cooks, including an extensive selection of molds. Use them for specialty molds.
36 East 31st Street
New York, NY 10016
800-473-0577
www.jbprince.com

N.Y. Cake & Baking

This New York store caters to professionals and home cooks, and as such has a wide selection of products such as sheet gelatin and fondant, as well as silicone baking mats and molds and a very large selection of cookie cutters of all shapes and sizes.
56 West 22nd Street
New York, NY 10010
212-675-CAKE
www.nycake.com

Index

Note: Page references in *italics* indicate recipe photographs.